Stockton & Billingham College
KT-381-936
4339501003098442772601 2
TECHNICAL COLLEGE

THE BATTLEMENT GARDEN

THE MIRROR OF BRITAIN SERIES

THE ISLAND SUNRISE: Prehistoric Britain
Jill Paton Walsh

BEYOND THE INHABITED WORLD: Roman Britain
Anthony Thwaite

GREEN BLADES RISING: The Anglo-Saxons
Kevin Crossley-Holland

A STRONG LAND AND A STURDY: England in the Middle Ages
Richard Barber

THE BATTLEMENT GARDEN:
Britain from the Wars of the Roses to the Age of Shakespeare
C. Walter Hodges

DRUMS AND TRUMPETS: The House of Stuart
Kirsty McLeod

THE HOUSE OF HANOVER: England in the 18th Century
Leon Garfield

A MIGHTY FERMENT: Britain in the Age of Revolution, 1750–1850
David Snodin

FOR QUEEN AND COUNTRY: Britain in the Victorian Age
Margaret Drabble

THE CRACK IN THE TEACUP: Britain in the Twentieth Century
Marina Warner

THE MIRROR OF BRITAIN SERIES
General Editor : Kevin Crossley-Holland

THE BATTLEMENT GARDEN

BRITAIN FROM THE WARS OF THE ROSES TO THE AGE OF SHAKESPEARE

C. Walter Hodges

ANDRE DEUTSCH

First published 1979 by
André Deutsch Limited
105 Great Russell Street London WC1

Set, printed and bound in Great Britain by
Fakenham Press Limited, Fakenham, Norfolk

Colour plates originated by
Keene Engraving Ltd, London
and printed by White Quill Press Ltd
Mitcham Surrey

British Library Cataloguing in Publication Data

Hodges, Cyril Walter
The battlement garden. – (Mirror of Britain series).
1. England – Civilization – 16th century – Juvenile literature
I. Title II. Series
942.05 DA320

ISBN 0-233-96938-1

For Laura

ACKNOWLEDGMENTS

Acknowledgments are due to the following for permission to reproduce the colour and black and white plates: J. Allan Cash, 14, 16; The Ashmolean Museum, Oxford, 10; The British Library, *1*, 3, 6, 9, 20, 25, 32, 40, 44, 46, 50, 53; Boymans-van-Beuningen Museum, Rotterdam, 31; The Trustees of the British Museum, 1; Cambridge University Collection, 12, 13; A. E. Coe and Sons, 34; College of Arms, *3*; The Courtauld Institute, 21, 24; The Department of the Environment, Crown Copyright, 23, 26; Mr Simon Wingfield Digby, Sherborne Castle, 57; Mary Evans Picture Library, 2, 48; Hampshire County Council, 19; Hayes Studio, Devon, 41; Kunsthistorisches Museum, Vienna, 5; Master and Fellows, Magdelene College, Cambridge, 39; The Mansell Collection, 7, 33, 36, 55; The National Maritime Museum, *6*, *8*; The National Monuments Record, 17(a); The National Portrait Gallery, *4*, 28, 42, 54; The National Trust, 15; Oxford University Press, 35, 51 (from *Shakespeare's Theatre* by C. Walter Hodges); Museo del Prado, Madrid, 27; The Science Museum, 18; The Trustees and Guardians of Shakespeare's Birthplace and the Governors and headmaster of King Edward VI School, Stratford-upon-Avon, 29; The Victoria and Albert Museum, *2*, *5*, *7*, 4, 8, 37, 45, 56. Copyright Reserved: 22, 38, 43.

Thanks are also due to Horst Kolo for photographing plates 11, 30, 47, 49, 52 and to Leonard Leone for photographing plate 17(b).

CONTENTS

Prologue: THE BATTLEMENT GARDEN

This other Eden, demi-paradise,
This fortress built by Nature for herself,
Against infection and the hand of war:
This happy breed of men, this little world,
This precious stone, set in the silver sea
Which serves it in the office of a wall . . .
RICHARD II ACT II. SC. i

A GARDEN paradise, protected by a castle wall from invasion by the wild and ruthless world outside: that was how William Shakespeare imagined the England of his day, towards the end of the Tudor century, in the last years of the reign of Queen Elizabeth I. In his own lifetime he had seen the garden become fruitful and the wall become strong. Such was the picture in his mind.

It was not a new picture. The old painters had always represented gardens as pretty places with orderly walks and flowers enclosed within a battlemented wall. The Garden of Eden itself was usually shown like that. When Adam and Eve were turned out of it, the gate in the wall was slammed behind them. They were out in the wild forest, the hostile world. The best they could then do was to dig and clear it, and make fields for the growing of their food. Mankind ever since has been trying to get back into the Garden.

England before the Tudor times was still very widely covered with forests and wild lands. Blotched out and spreading into all these were the pastures and field lands, with paths joining them from village to village, and roads of a sort – a muddy, rutted sort, mostly – from town to town. And from point to point over the whole country, on lonely cliffs, or at the bends of rivers or at strong points above the towns, stood the towered castles. From these the great lords who had owned the country ever since it had been divided among their ancestors at the Norman Conquest, four hundred years before, rode out from time to time with their forces to make their own alliances with or against other great lords, or for or against the king, according to their powers or their interests. Meanwhile at home in the castles, as in the market towns below them, an ordinary life went on, and here and there within the walls the ladies of the castle found space to lay out their little gardens, for medicinal herbs or flowers; and along the wider spaces of the battlements they would put tubs for pansies and rose trees (see colour plate 1). It made a pleasant walk around the walls of a summer evening. After all, the number of battles and sieges which most castles had to sustain was mercifully few. There was time and peace enough to cultivate some roses.

Not that, in England, roses were an emblem of peace in those days. Far from it. The Wars of the Roses is the name given to a merciless series of conflicts which began in 1455 and went on for thirty years (see plate 1). Under the badges of either the white rose of York, or the red rose of Lancaster, the nobles of these two great factions battled against each other for the power to claim and crown the King of England, each for his own side. By the time they had done slaying each other for that privilege up and down the land, most of the noble families of England had wiped each other out, and the whole land was covered in dead battlefields.

However, as usually happens, after the warring armies had trampled through the countryside, the ordinary people closed in again over the scars and continued their ordinary life as best they could. Law and order, of a sort, were somehow kept going. A certain troublesome gentleman in Warwickshire, who had on several occasions set out to disturb the peace on his own account, was caught and put in prison for it. His name was Sir Thomas Malory. While in prison he occupied his time by writing down everything he could find or remember of the old legends of King Arthur and

1. War ravages the countryside. Woodcut by Albrecht Dürer, 1515.

his Knights of the Round Table. It grew into a long book. He finished writing it in 1470, and gave it the title *Morte d'Arthur*. In that work the world of high chivalry and lordly castles which, whatever its reality may have been, was now coming to an end on its own battlefields, was finally enclosed and preserved in the figures of romance.

At about the same time another Englishman, William Caxton, who had spent a prosperous life as a cloth merchant in the Netherlands, retired from that occupation to devote himself to what he most loved, the study of literature. Besides this, he had become fascinated by an invention he had seen being used in the Rhineland – a new sort of press for printing books, with moveable type. He bought one of these presses for himself, and came back with it to England. There, in Westminster, he set up as a printer (see plate 2). The news of the remarkable invention quickly spread. The Yorkist king Edward IV came with his courtiers to Caxton's printing shop, to see the press at work. We may be sure that few if any of these visitors could have imagined what a huge revolution in human affairs was contained in that simple little machine, as

2. An early printing press. The man on the right is setting up a line of type on his 'stick'. The man on the left is preparing the inking pads. The man pulling the lever is applying the pressure. (*See also* plate 48.)

the oak-tree is contained in the acorn. Caxton himself could hardly have guessed. But on the day in 1476 when the first printed sheet was pulled from his press in Westminster, the old world of the Middle Ages in England came to an end, and the doors of the modern world began to open.

Two things happened in the year 1485 which, though at first they may seem very distant from each other, have an interesting connection. The first was that in that year William Caxton published the first printed edition of Sir Thomas Malory's *Morte d'Arthur* (see plate 3). The second was the battle of Bosworth, where the Wars of the Roses were brought to an end by the defeat and death of King Richard III. Now in his place Henry Tudor, the Earl of Richmond, became king with the title of Henry VII. The connection between these two events, as we shall see, was the legend of King Arthur.

3. King Arthur and Queen Guinevere watching a tournament. Woodcut from the second edition of *Morte d'Arthur*, printed by Wynkyn de Worde, Caxton's successor, in 1529.

KING ARTHUR'S LAND

IT is not usually supposed that Henry VII (see plate 4), the first Tudor monarch, had a fanciful or romantic disposition. On the contrary, he was a shrewd, realistic and calculating man, and it was with those qualities that he began the task of healing and uniting a country which had been disordered by thirty years of war between those great families who were supposed to have been governing it. But Henry Tudor was also a Welshman. He had been brought up in Wales, with a background of Welsh traditional culture. One of the chief heroes of that culture is King Arthur. The Arthurian legends are themselves nearly all of Celtic, that is Welsh, origin, and their earliest sources are in the Welsh language. Henry's family claimed to be descended from Arthur. When, during his boyhood, Henry had become heir to the Lancastrian succession, and so in danger of being hunted down and killed by the Yorkists, he had been taken for safety overseas to Britanny, another Celtic country where the stories of King Arthur and his knights were still preserved. So throughout his youth the old legend was a familiar part of his background. An important feature in that legend is that King Arthur never died, but only lies sleeping somewhere in the mystic Vale of Avalon, awaiting a time when his country, the whole realm of Britain, will need him again; and then he will awaken and return to it, and heal all its wounds and unite it under his beneficent rule. Doubtless with just such a thought in mind, and certainly with a similar task in hand after the Wars of the Roses, Henry Tudor, when he came to the throne set about the task of uniting his country.

4. Henry VII. Contemporary portrait bust by Pietro Torrigiano.

His first step was to make Elizabeth of York his queen, thus uniting the houses of York and Lancaster by marriage under a new badge, a united rose of equal red and white. And when their first son, the new Prince of Wales, was born, he was named Arthur. It was a promise for the future. Henry did not see himself in the part of King Arthur, but he intended that after he had put his kingdom in good order once more, and healed its wounds, a new King Arthur should succeed him and bring in a new Golden Age.

He also intended that the new Arthurian Kingdom should have powerful friends abroad. That could be arranged by marriage. So

5. Portrait of Catherine of Aragon in her youth by Miguel Sittow.

before he was even two years old, the little Prince Arthur was betrothed to the little Princess Catherine of Aragon who was nearly three, the youngest daughter of King Ferdinand of Aragon and Queen Isabella of Castille. The marriage of Ferdinand and Isabella had united Spain just as the marriage of King Henry with Elizabeth of York had united Britain. A marriage of England and Spain promised well for the future. There was some difficult haggling between the monarchs of the two countries about Catherine's dowry, but in the end even that was settled, and in the course of time, when the two young people were considered old enough (Arthur was nearly fifteen) the future Princess of Wales (see plate 5) set sail from Spain for England, to be married.

The Spaniards were at that time, with the Portuguese, the most experienced seafarers in the world. It was only nine years since Christopher Columbus had sailed in Spanish ships to the far side of the Atlantic Ocean; and Catherine had herself been present, a little girl, when the great navigator had returned in triumph to the court of her father and mother, bringing with him the strange animals and savage men he had discovered in the new world on the far side of the Ocean. The ships of the squadron which was now escorting Catherine to England were not very different from those Columbus himself had used. She would naturally have sailed in the best and largest of them. It would have been of the type called a carrack, about 100 feet long and 20 broad, heavy and tubby, with three masts and large square sails. These were not yet the days of the great Spanish galleons. The voyage to England took six weeks, the little ships rolling about in heavy weather, once, even, having to put back to port for shelter and repair. But at long last they sighted the coast of Devonshire (see plate 6). Catherine of Aragon came ashore at Plymouth at the beginning of October, 1501. Her progress from there to London, a journey of little more than two hundred miles, lasted three weeks.

A 'progress' (see plate 7) was the name given to an official journey by a great or royal personage. In those days kings and queens were frequently on the move from one part of a country to another, to be seen by as many of their people as possible, and to enjoy the hospitality of their wealthier noblemen. Since great

6. The south-western approaches to England in the sixteenth century. An early map by Theodore de Bry. Note the profile sketches of the coastlines, to aid recognition from the sea.

The saide Iles, when they lye South East from you abouts two leagues
The Easterne Coast of Englands ende when it lyeth East North East from you three leagues
The Lizard or Cape of Cornewall as it appeareth when the West ende thereof lyeth North West from you aleague, and the East ende North two leagues
Falemouth, when the Castell lyeth North West & by West from you; And Dudmans poynt North from you, three leagues
Dudman poynt
GLIÆ PARS
Milbrooke
Edgcome
Plymmouth
S. Nicholas
Foye
Tallant poynt
Dudman poynt
Falmouth hauen
Ide stone
Mewstone
SEPTENTRIO
ENGLAND AND FRAVNCE
ORIENS
English leagues 20 in a degree
Spanishe leagues 17½ in a degree
Dutche leagues 15 in a degree

7. A royal progress, as shown in a French tapestry of about 1573. The progress of Catherine of Aragon through England in 1501 would have been very similar

8. Sheep and shepherds, from an embroidered table covering (the 'Bradford Table Carpet' made in the late sixteenth century). Note the wolf running off with the lamb.

people always travelled with a large following of courtiers and officials, with their servants and secretaries, with heralds riding ahead, with an armed guard, and a long train of baggage waggons behind, a royal progress was like the march of a small army, and the hospitality given along the way was very costly to the giver. The arrival of a Spanish princess who was to be the future Queen of England was a state event, attended by every sort of honour. The High Steward of England had been sent by the King to supervise each stage of the journey. Gentlemen from every county she passed through joined her progress to accompany it along their own part of the way. The Spanish ambassador had come from London with his interpreters, for neither the princess nor her attendants at that time spoke any English. But official speeches of welcome, such as those she listened to at Exeter, after her long

9. Ploughing, sowing and harrowing. From a calendar of the early sixteenth century.

day's journey from Plymouth, over foul roads through what was then a wild county at the far end of England, were usually given in Latin, which she might have understood, in spite of the strong Devonshire accent in which they were spoken.

Exeter was the first notable town she saw in England, and by the route she travelled she saw no other till she reached London. The greenness of the countryside was like nothing she had ever seen before, and on the hills and downlands she saw more sheep and fatter (see plate 8), than there were in any other country in Europe. The fields around the villages were laid out in long strips with very few hedges and ploughed by wooden ploughs drawn by oxen or horses (see plate 9), as had been done everywhere in the western world since the most ancient times. Cattle were tethered on the fallow strips, or on the common lands beyond the fields, and watched over by the older village children. As in Spain, there were many windmills. Roads everywhere along Catherine's journey were very bad, boggy and slow because of recent rain, so that the horses sometimes could not pull the waggons and the job had to be done by oxen. Occasionally, however, they would come upon many miles of firm road where the old paving stones which the Romans had laid down a thousand years before were still under the surface, not yet dug up and carried away for house or farm building. Along that road in the peaceful south of England she saw no castles, but many beautiful churches even in small villages, with carved stonework such as in her own country was only to be found in proud cathedrals; and there were many rich abbeys and monasteries. Holy Church was one of the wealthiest landowners in the country. The stopping places of her journey were usually at great abbeys such as Sherborne, which possessed large and suitable guest-houses. She stayed at the Benedictine nunneries of Shaftesbury and Amesbury. On the way to Amesbury she passed within sight of Stonehenge. People said these huge stones had been put there by magic, perhaps by old Merlin in King Arthur's time, and that it was from one of these stones that Arthur had drawn out the sword Excalibur. People are often confused in such matters.

King Henry and Prince Arthur came with a royal escort to greet the princess at a village some miles outside London. Soon after, she made her state entry into the city. Looking behind all the flags and banners hung out to welcome her under the autumn sky, she may have thought the narrow-streeted, half-timbered, high-storied, crowded city was a dark sort of place, compared with her bright, sun-baked Spain, which she had left behind her forever. Nevertheless London was already one of the richest cities in Europe. It was governed by a convocation of guilds of wealthy merchant-tradesmen, and the Lord Mayor whom they elected every year ruled with the authority of a great prince. It was a city with a population (at the time of Catherine's arrival) of about 75,000, and the number was increasing rapidly. To accommodate the overflow, houses were already being built beyond the walls, along the roads out of the seven gates, and across the river at the other end of the famous bridge with its nineteen arches, itself built up with houses from end to end. Looking at the city from that

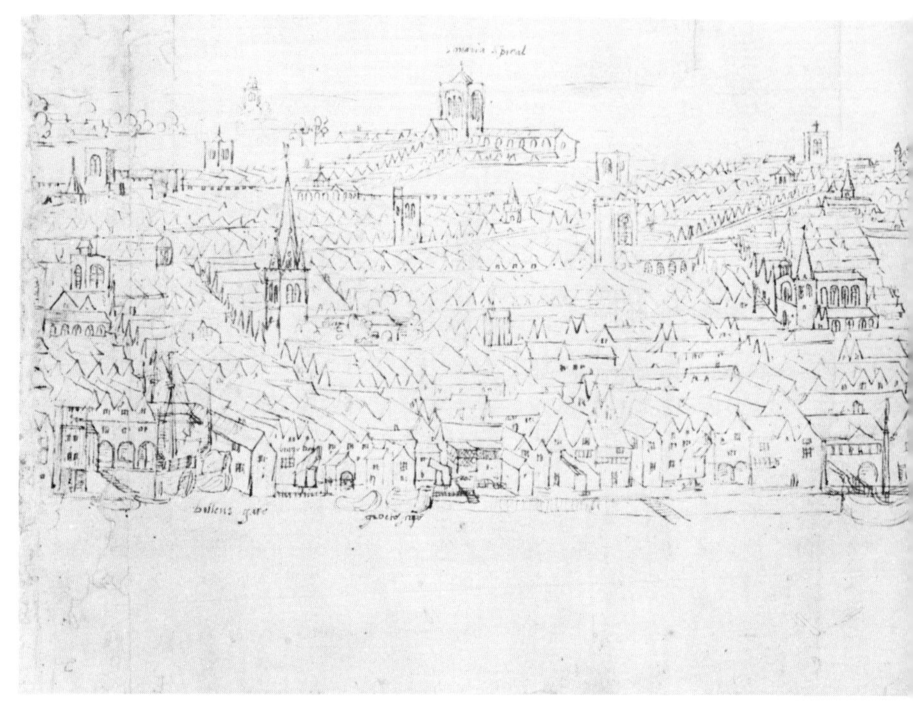

10. Drawings from the sketchbooks of Antony Wyngaerde, c. 1545. These are the earliest known pictures of old London. (*Above*) The riverside from Billingsgate to the Tower of London (note Traitor's Gate, Tower Hill and the scaffold). (*Right*) Old St Paul's.

other side (see plate 10) Catherine saw the river frontage of wharfs and warehouses which were the source of so much wealth; the two fortresses, Baynards Castle and the Tower of London, which guarded each end of the old city wall where it met the river; and above the crowded thousands of tiled roofs – for thatch, the common roofing material outside, was not permitted in London for fear of fire – were the clusters of spires and towers which proclaimed only a part of the 150 churches in the city below. Their bells were all ringing as Catherine's procession entered across the bridge. High up above all the rest, five hundred feet into the air, stood the lofty spire of St Paul's Cathedral where, a few days later, Prince Arthur and Princess Catherine were married.

That being done and the feasting over, the young couple left London, and took to the road again. Once more the horses, the heralds, the baggage-waggons and the cavaliers, another royal progress, another route. Arthur was Prince of Wales, and so to Wales he must now go with his bride, to set up his princely court at Ludlow Castle. They went by way of Warwickshire, which is the heart of England, and so on through the Forest of Arden, just south of where the great city of Birmingham now is. They were at Ludlow for Christmas. How pleasant it would have been there, beside the river Severn in the summer time, with the prince's banner curling out in a little breeze above the castle keep. But that summer did not bring such pleasure. In April, from what sickness we do not know, the young prince suddenly died. So ended Henry Tudor's plan for a new King Arthur; and so the Princess Catherine of Aragon became a widow at sixteen.

SEVERAL AND CHAMPION: LIFE IN THE COUNTRY

THE people of the Forest of Arden who had stood along the roadside to watch Prince Arthur and his bride pass by on their way to Ludlow, went back to their cottages with plenty to talk about round their Christmas firesides. Such fine horses, such heavy-loaded waggons, such splendid clothes and trappings, such banners! Those embroideries on the curtains of the horse-litter were the royal arms of Aragon. She in the litter was the Spanish princess. And so on: 'What great ones do, the less will prattle of', wrote Shakespeare in *Twelfth Night*. It is a quotation in season, for it was on Twelfth Night that the twelve days of the Christmas festival came to an end. After that brief interval the countryman's year of toil began. January and February were hard and hungry months in the country. All the animals that could be spared had been butchered in November (see plate 11), the beef joints salted down in tubs, the pork hung up to cure in the smoke of the chimney. There was never enough fodder to keep many animals through a whole winter. Those that could be kept for work or breeding, when other food became scarce, were fed on the loppings from the trees, as the woodlands were cleared for firewood. They ate leaves, mosses, ivies and young shoots. Nothing was wasted, everything was picked clean to the ground in Tudor husbandry. In January the lean cattle were out pulling the ploughs and harrows. It was lambing time, time for sowing oats and beans, time for snaring rabbits and keeping the henroost safe from hungry foxes.

11. November: killing the pig. From a series of engravings of the twelve months by Crispin van der Passe.

In spring people coming back from the markets at Warwick and Stratford brought the news they had heard there. The young prince had died. The women said alas, poor souls, thinking not only of the Prince, but of the Spanish princess. What would happen to her now? Would she be sent home to Spain? Then the talk turned back again to their own Warwickshire matters.

Warwickshire is a county divided in half, diagonally from north-east to south-west, by the river Avon. In Tudor times the two halves were very different from each other in character. The north-western half was called Arden. Until very recently it had been all forest. It was in fact the forest of Arden, of Shakespeare's play *As You Like It*. Now, however, it was slowly being cleared and settled, though it was still densely wooded in many places. The south-eastern half was called Feldon, or Fielden. It was laid out for cultivation, without hedges or fences, from village to village, in those enormous open fields that had been customary since very early times (see plate 12). Every village had three of these fields, two of which were sown while the third lay fallow, to rest and recover the fertility of its soil. Each field lay fallow for a year, in turn. All the fields were divided into long strips for cultivation, and all the village families had their allotted number of strips, not all together but in different parts of the common field, so that all had a share between the better and the less good parts of the soil. The strips themselves were usually of a length that had been established by an ancient and useful practice: they were as long as

12. 'Champion' or 'open-field' cultivation: a modern example in Laxton, Nottinghamshire.

the distance a pair of oxen could plough a furrow without tiring themselves to a halt; at which point they turned and ploughed the next furrow, back again. The oxen had decided, on average, that the distance was 220 yards, which we still call (or did until very recently when the metric measurements came in) a furrow-long, or furlong. The strips were about 30 yards wide, and were divided from each other by narrow grassy pathways called 'balks'. A large village might be surrounded by more than a thousand of these strips. The villagers not only had their shares in the common fields, but often shared the ploughs and other farm implements as well. It meant that all had to work by common agreement, as a community. Such agreements are not easy to change once they have been made, which meant in its turn that there was little chance of bringing in many new ideas (such as the common planting of a new or untried crop), because the number of new ideas which everybody will accept, all together at any one time, is usually very few.

Outside the area of the common lands were the estates of gentlemen or yeomen freeholders. Further away was the great house of the lord of the manor and its demesne. The fields of such wealthy landowners were worked by their tenants, either for pay or in lieu of rent. But the landowners were better able to make up their own minds about the most profitable use of their land, and in Tudor times it had become clear to increasing numbers of them that the open-field system was a hindrance to their prosperity. The way to wealth was to enclose their lands with hedges (see plate 13), so that cattle could graze untended, and new, late-ripening crops, such as turnips, could be grown without danger of being rooted up by the village cattle, which in the common fields were put out to graze on the strips (thus also manuring the land after the harvest). Enclosed land also meant there were fewer labourers to pay. During the whole of the Tudor period the enclosure of land in all parts of the country was making continual encroachment upon the common fields. The commoners complained and resisted, sometimes with violence. The movement for enclosure was thus delayed in places, but little by little the enclosures continued. Smallholding labourers were turned out of their homes to make

13. 'Several' or 'enclosed' fields as they remain today, near Bourton-on-the-Hill, Gloucestershire.

way for enclosed pastures, and for the first time the country began to be afflicted by an increasing number of poor, unemployed people.

Country under the open-field system was called 'champion' (from the Old French word 'champagne', meaning open country). Enclosed fields were called 'several' (severed, or set apart). In the end 'several' was bound to win, because it was in itself a better method of farming. The countryman poet Thomas Tusser, in a poem called 'A Comparison between Champion Country and Several', wrote:

Good land that is several, crops may have three,
In champion country it may not so be . . .

Against this we may set the complaint of another writer, who observed: 'Where forty person had their livings, now one man and his shepherd hath all.'

English wool and English woollen cloth were the best in the world. In the preceding century the export of woollen goods had brought great wealth to English merchants, and in Tudor times the trade increased. It all came from the backs of English sheep. Foreign visitors were astonished at the number of sheep in England. From the hills of Cumberland and Yorkshire, to the Sussex and Berkshire Downs, on Salisbury Plain and the Cotswolds, wherever you went in England you would find great flocks of sheep with their shepherds. Likewise in all parts of the country you would find weavers at work in their cottages. Nick Bottom, the play-acting weaver of *A Midsummer Night's Dream* was one such. In other trades the craftsmen had found it convenient and more profitable to group themselves together in the towns, under the rule of their trade guilds. The weaving trade had reversed this, and had returned to the country districts near the sheep-folds, becoming what still is sometimes called a 'cottage industry'.

Enclosure was making it possible to bring sheep down into lowland pastures, as could not well be done in 'champion' country. In Warwickshire the Forest of Arden was being cleared by yeoman farmers who could enclose their land at will, since it had never been champion and there could be no complaint, as there would have been across the river in Feldon. So the farmers of Arden became prosperous, being able to manage their lands between pasture and arable, as suited them best. One of these was a certain Thomas Arden of Wilmcote. His family had been in the Arden country so long that nobody knew which had had the name first. We may imagine him in the year 1509, a middle-aged man walking home to Wilmcote from Stratford with his son Robert. Thomas Arden had prospered, and had just bought more land in the village of Snitterfield nearby. He was having some oak trees felled there, and had just been to the tanner, Master Field of

1. A rose garden on the battlements.
Illustration from the *Roman de la Rose*. Flemish, 15th c.

2. April in the fields. Enlarged detail from a 16th c. miniature by Simon Beninck.

Stratford, to sell the bark. Tanners customarily used oak bark for the processing of skins. The heartwood of the oaks would go for building. Smaller trees and loppings would be taken up by the charcoal burners, of whom there were many, always busy at their smokey work in the forest clearings of Arden. They sold their charcoal to the iron and steel workers twenty miles away in Birmingham. Though it was hardly more than a scattered village, Birmingham was even then becoming a centre for metal work. Its many forges turned out swords and knives, bits and buckles and stirrups for saddlery, and hammers and nails. The axes that were felling Thomas Arden's trees came from there. He could reckon that the sale of his timber would pay for the clearing of the ground, and when that was done he would enclose it and put sheep on it. It should be very profitable.

14. The Arden family house at Wilmcote, as it is today.

Back home again at his Wilmcote house (see plate 14), Thomas told his wife all the news he had heard at Stratford. The King in London had died, and his younger son had come to the throne as Henry VIII. But more than that: the new king had at once announced his decision to marry the Princess Catherine, his brother Arthur's widow. In the seven years since Prince Arthur's death she had lived a life of patient uncertainty, being held as if she were a hostage, while her royal Spanish father and her royal English father-in-law wrangled endlessly about her dowry, which had not yet been handed over. Now she was to become Queen of England after all. The dowry was eventually paid.

The Arden family were nevertheless a little puzzled by the whole event. Was it permissable for a man, even a king, to marry his brother's widow? They were reassured to learn that in this case the pope in Rome had specially allowed it. It was permissable.

HOUSE AND HOME

THE Arden family house was, like most houses in Tudor England built on a framework of good oak. Timber was still abundant, though the great English forests, such as that of Arden, were at least showing signs of thinning out, with so much demand being made upon them, not only for house-building, but for ships also, and especially for fuel for the smelting of iron. The iron foundries of Sussex were rapidly depleting the forest of the Weald, just as the Birmingham foundries were beginning to make inroads upon Arden.

In timber-framed houses the spaces in the frame were usually filled with a 'wattle' of twigs or withies, such as hazel, plaited together, and this was covered with a generous 'daub' of clay or mud. Cover the wattle-and-daub with plaster inside and out, and there you had a good wall. You could have it pretty or plain. Many houses were simply whitewashed all over, timber and all. Others, built for more show and stylishness, especially in the later times when life was becoming easier, took advantage of the possibilities offered by the timber framework to work it deliberately into patterns of fascinating variety. A famous example, still standing, is Little Moreton Hall in Cheshire (see plate 15). Well-to-do people liked also to enrich their timbers with ornamental carving, and to use colours on the plaster spaces between, instead of mere whitewash. The effect of such houses, grouped together in the town streets, could be very pleasing.

After timber, the commonest building material was stone. In

15. The pattern of Tudor building in timber: Little Moreton Hall in Cheshire. An inscription over one of the windows says: 'Richard Dale, carpenter, made this window by the Grace of God'.

some parts of the country there was more stone than wood. But strangely enough, what was not at all common for use in ordinary houses, certainly not at the beginning of the Tudor century, was brick. The Roman brick-works had long been forgotten. However, the art of brickmaking was being revived, and by the time of Henry VIII bricks were being used as a rather splendid material for the building of grand houses and palaces, such as Hampton Court. Because they were also a very convenient material they were eagerly sought after, as supplies became more available, especially for the building of chimneys.

Proper, well-built chimneys, in Henry VIII's time, in ordinary people's houses, were still a luxury. In country cottages, and even in some town houses, the mediaeval louvre, a sort of hole in the roof to let out the smoke from the hearth below, was still to be seen. In most houses the family hearthstone was set against a stone wall, with a canopy over it and a flue to carry the smoke away as well as possible, but there was usually no proper chimney *stack*, and without that the smoke might easily blow back into the room again, or low-flying sparks set fire to a nearby thatch. However, with the greater availability of bricks, and the increasing prosperity of the nation, the people of Tudor England began to make their homes more comfortable in ways that had not been dreamed of in earlier times, and one sign of this was a general enthusiasm for the building of chimneys. A country clergyman named William Harrison, who in 1577 published a book describing life in England in his time, said that there were old men still living in his village who noted that one of the things most 'marvellously altered' in their lifetimes was 'the multitude of chimneys lately erected, whereas in their young days there was not above two or three, if so many, in most towns of the realm (the religious houses and manor places of their lords always excepted, and peradventure some great personages). . . .' It was part of what Harrison described as 'the great amendment of lodging'. The improvement in ordinary home life, at which these old men marvelled so much in the later part of the century, included even such simple comforts as mere bedding. 'Our fathers, and we ourselves', said they, 'have lien full oft upon straw pallets, covered only with a sheet under coverlets made of dagswain* and hop-harlots, and a good round log under their heads instead of a bolster. And if so that our fathers or the good man of the house had a mattress or flockbed, and thereto a sack of chaff to rest his head upon, he thought himself to be as well lodged as the lord of the town.' Even to have a bedchamber to oneself was a luxury, a privilege usually enjoyed only by the master and mistress of the house. The rest of the household shared the available space in the few communal rooms, the hall, the kitchen, the attic, men in this place, women in that, several to a bed, whatever the bed might be. In winter they crowded together to keep warm (see plate 16). It must have been like life on a long voyage in a small ship.

* 'I use their own terms,' adds Harrison. Dagswain and hop-harlots were kinds of very coarse cloth.

16. The family hearth at the Ardens' house, Wilmcote, as seen today. Probably the old family would hardly recognize it in this tidy and well-furnished state.

Of course one knows about all this; one has heard it all before, about the primitive nature of life in earlier times; but it is well to keep it in mind, that for most people in Tudor times even so simple a piece of furniture as a wooden armchair with a back to it was a luxury reserved only for the head of the household. Everyone else sat on backless benches and stools. Ordinary domestic pots and pans, kettles and candlesticks, were valuable things which a provident householder would take care to mention in his will, bequeathing them item by item to his wife and family. With such simple things in mind we can better understand the value of all that chimney-building. It was the best thing that had happened since glass had become cheap enough for most people to have it in at least some of their windows. As the Tudor times went on, glazed windows were becoming common everywhere. And now, with these good new chimneys and a house free from soot and smoke, people could at last begin to think of having clean walls in pleasantly kept rooms. One could have a greater number of fireplaces in the house, and so a greater number of smaller rooms, warmer and more private. It was no wonder the Tudor chimney builders made such a proud show of them, carving the bricks in their stacks into fanciful and elaborate shapes (see plate 17).

Smaller and more private rooms. Privacy itself is perhaps one of the greatest (though least noticed) of real luxuries. Even at the best of Tudor times, even in the best and grandest of houses, there was very little of it; for even with the greater number of smaller rooms, those rooms usually had no outside corridor, but led each from one into the next, so that people were passing in and out, to and fro, most of the time. The greater the house the greater the household, with all its servants and secretaries and maids and pages. Indoors, especially in winter-time, everybody lived in a great social hugger-mugger. The natural joy of Spring was therefore doubly joyful for people to whom the return of the warm sunshine and the sheltering leaves meant, after all those dark winter months, that they could if they wished get away for a while from the noisy, crowded house (see colour plate 2). Lovers, for instance, could wander off into the woods and be alone. Simply to be private at last was, so to speak, a lyrical gift of nature, and it is no wonder so much poetry was written in praise of Spring.

If it was a luxury to be private it was a still greater luxury to be clean. A clean house, a clean body and clean clothes were luxuries few people could afford the time and energy to keep up altogether, try as they might. Those chimneys, however, as they were increasingly built, helped. With no more soot hanging on walls and ceilings, people could find it more worth while to lay out money for the comfort and decoration of their rooms. Walls were decorated with colour washes, or with painted patterns, or hung with painted cloths (woven tapestries were best of all, but were of course too expensive for any but the richest people). Wooden panelling, sometimes with carved detail in 'linenfold' designs was coming into fairly general use. It kept out the damp and kept in

a

b

17. Tudor chimneys of carved brick. (a) Layer Marney gatehouse, Essex. (b) Compton Wynyates, Warwickshire.

the warmth, and could be dusted down and polished by the maids. But once again the larger the house the more numerous were the servants, and the more people there were, the more dirt and difficulty they created of themselves. Think only of the lavatory problem in a large Tudor household. (It was an Elizabethan gentleman, Sir John Harington, who invented a domestic water-closet (see plate 18), for which the whole modern world may thank him; but it was another three hundred years before it became possible to bring such a thing into general use.) The difficulties of somehow getting oneself washed, the very soap having been made in one's own kitchen; of taking a bath (not so very often); of cleaning one's teeth with a soapy rag; of keeping oneself smelling nice by the use of perfumed waters for which, like the soap, the lady of the house had her own recipes; to say nothing of the constant war against fleas and vermin; these decencies were all only kept going by continuous efforts of disciplined refinement and determination. The efforts did succeed, however, At any rate it seems that English homes were sweeter and cleaner places at the end of the Tudor age than at the beginning. In the earlier days, in Henry's time, the great scholar Erasmus came to England to visit his friend Sir Thomas More, and he was shocked at the dirty way in which so many of the people he met kept their houses. In particular, he was disgusted by the floors, which were strewn over with rushes and herbs, a pleasant custom one might think, except that (in his understanding) they were not swept out for twenty years, but were full of spittle, dogs' mess and table garbage, all which, when it became offensive, was simply strewn over with more rushes. Was that true? If so, things were very different fifty years later when another visitor, a Dutch doctor, described the English as follows: '. . . the neat cleanliness, the exquisite fineness, the pleasant and delightful furniture in every point for household, wonderfully reposed me; their chambers and parlours strewed over with sweet herbs refreshed me; their nosegays finely intermingled with sundry sorts of fragrant flowers in their bedchambers and privy rooms, with comfortable smell cheered me up and entirely delighted all my senses.'

At the end of the century William Harrison was describing the

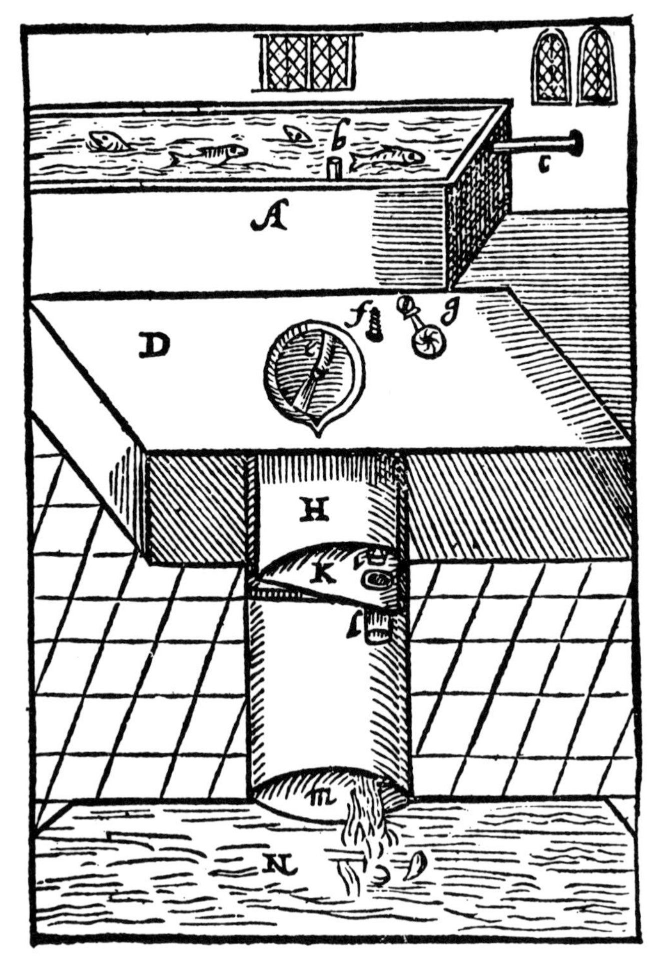

A. the Cesterne.
B. the little washer.
C. the wast pipe.
D. the seate boord.
E. the pipe that comes from the Cesterne.
F. the Screw.
G. the Scallop shell to cover it when it is shut downe.[53]
H. the stoole pot.
I. the stopple.
K. the current.
L. the sluce.[54]
M. N. the vault into which it falles: alwayes remember that (   )[55] at noone and at night, emptie it and leave it halfe a foote deepe in fayre water. And this being well done, and orderly kept, your worst privie may be as sweet as your best chamber.

18. Sir John Harington's lavatory: a diagram from his book on how to build it, with a modern reconstruction drawing showing how it might have looked when set up.

homes of English gentlemen and merchants as having 'a great profusion of tapestry, Turkey work, pewter, brass, fine linen, and thereto costly cupboards of plate, worth five or six hundred or a thousand pounds . . .' And all such wealth and comfort, Harrison went on, 'is descended yet lower unto the inferior artificers and many farmers, who have learned also to garnish their cupboards with plate, and their beds with tapestry and silk hangings, and their tables with fine napery . . .'

Was it true about the 'inferior artificers and many farmers'? For example, did Thomas Arden of Wilmcote really furnish his bed with tapestry and silk? We may well doubt it. Harrison was most likely exaggerating, to make his point, which was (never mind the silk hangings and such) that during his lifetime in Tudor England the comforts of a truly civilized standard of living, even as we understand them today, had begun to find their way into the lives and homes of ordinary men and women.

THE KING'S REVOLUTION

IN the great hall of Winchester castle there hangs on the wall a huge round table of painted wood (see plate 19), long said to be the very one used by King Arthur and his knights, in the castle of Camelot. In fact, as has only recently been detected, it seems to have been made for Edward III, for an order of chivalry he intended to found in the manner of King Arthur. The idea later bore fruit, only a little changed, when he founded the Order of the Garter in its place. On the round table at Winchester, at the position where 'King Arthur' should sit, is painted the picture of a king, possibly at one time a portrait of King Edward III himself. But in Henry VIII's time that was painted over. What we now see is a picture of Henry VIII. It seems that when that king came to the throne he not only married his brother Arthur's young widow, Catherine of Aragon, but he also inherited his father's idea that the Tudors should unite the realm under a new King Arthur. Only he would now have to play the part of Arthur himself.

The treasures and pleasures of King Henry's court must indeed have seemed at the time like a new Camelot. We read of his famous palace of Nonesuch, in Surrey (see plate 20), built and decorated for him by architects, painters and sculptors from all over Europe. It was described by Samuel Pepys, who visited it in the late seventeenth century shortly before it was demolished, and there remain a few pictures of it, showing its fantastic ornamental towers with their gilded roofs, vanes and crestings, and the privy

19. 'King Arthur's' round table in Winchester Castle. Note the Tudor Rose in the centre.
Inset: detail, showing Henry VIII as King Arthur.

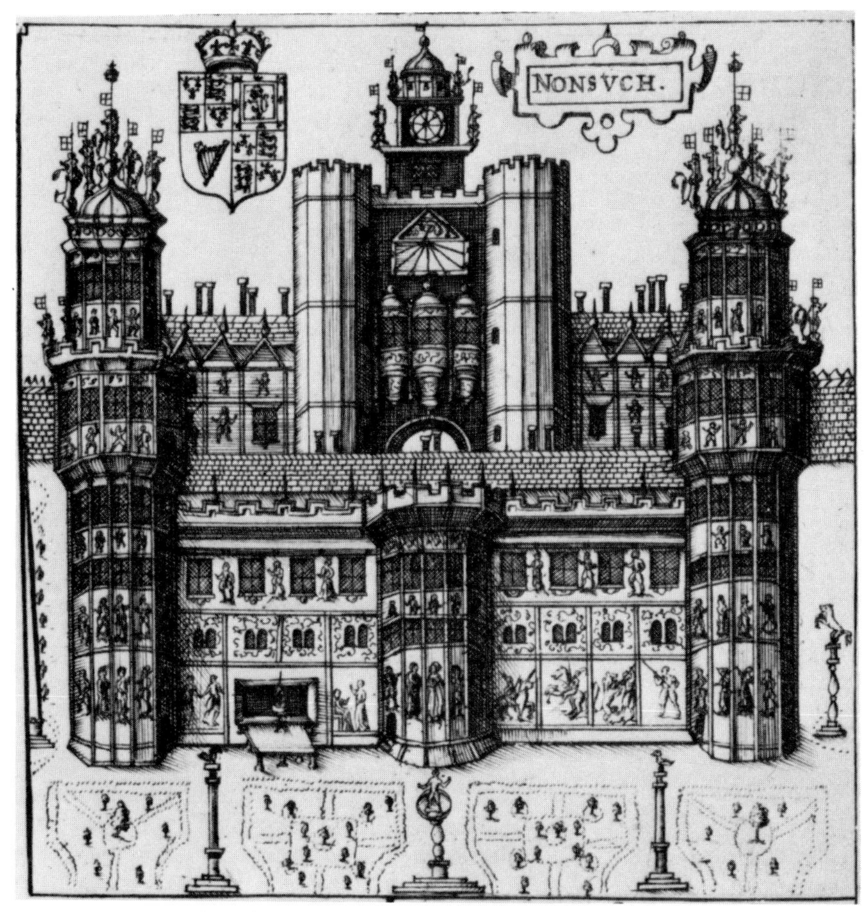

20. Nonesuch Palace in Surrey. From a contemporary engraving by Jodocus Hondius.

garden with its walks and its fountain with the stone pelican, and (says Pepys) 'two other marble pinnacles or pyramids, called the Falcon perches, betwixt which is placed a fountain of white marble with a lead cistern, which fountain is set round with six trees called lilac trees, which trees bear no fruit, but only a most pleasant flower.' Among such garden walks in the shade of the lilacs, strolled the poets, painters and musicians who were welcomed at King Henry's court. It was like the coming of a long-delayed spring. The Renaissance of European culture which had

21. Henry VIII. Painting by Hans Holbein.

3. Henry VIII jousting at Westminster, with Catherine of Aragon and her ladies looking on.

4. The young Queen Elizabeth I in her coronation robes.

begun in Italy and spread slowly northwards by way of France into the Netherlands, had now at last crossed over into England. Henry VIII was the first English monarch to take a deliberate part in that Renaissance, and to invite foreign artists to his court. In the first year of his reign he sent for the Italian sculptor Pietro Torrigiano (who is famous among other things for having broken the nose of Michelangelo in a fight) to design and make the figures for the tomb of Henry VII and his queen in Westminster Abbey, where they are still to be seen. He later invited Hans Holbein from Switzerland, to be his court painter. The superb pictures which Holbein drew and painted of the king (see plate 21) and the men and women of his court are among the most splendid records in portraiture of any royal court in the world's history.

An English school of painting took a long while to establish, and in the beginning continued to rely greatly upon the help of foreign artists. But English poetry was a native growth, and the Tudor court provided a warm soil for it to flourish in. Even here, however, there was a certain influence from Italy. It was Sir Thomas Wyatt (see plate 22) in King Henry's time who first introduced into England an Italian verse-form called the sonnet, which at the end of the century was to find its fullest expression in the hands of Shakespeare. The poems which Wyatt wrote in his native English manner are elegant and wistful, often addressed to beautiful, shadowy young women who have misunderstood and gently deserted him. His fortunes have 'turned into a strange fashion of forsaking'. His poetry has a graceful wit like a melancholy game played in a beautiful garden:

Forget not yet the great assays,
The cruel wrong, the scornful ways,
The painful patience in denays,
Forget not yet!

Forget not yet, forget not this,
How long ago hath been, and is
The mind that never meant amiss,
Forget not yet!

Forget not then thine own approved,
The which so long hath thee so loved,
Whose steadfast faith yet never moved;
Forget not this!

22. Sir Thomas Wyatt. Drawing by Hans Holbein.

There was also (we can do no more here than mention it) the marvellous, crackling poetry of John Skelton ('Ragged, tattered and jagged, rudely rainbeaten, rusty and moth-eaten') with which he satirized high and low in the land, from the mighty Cardinal Wolsey to the blowsy old ale-wife of Leatherhead, Eleanor Rumming.

At court, also, this was a time for splendid entertainments called 'masques' and 'interludes' which were presented to accompany great banquets. Masques were a form of ceremonial dance by torchlight, with extravagant disguising costumes. It was a fashion which the king copied from the ducal courts of Italy. Interludes were short plays, often written by poets (there is one by Skelton) and acted by players who were usually what we would call amateurs. Sometimes they were acted by the choirboys of the Chapel Royal. Many of these interludes were written by a certain John Heywood. He was married to the daughter of a printer who himself wrote plays, and printed them. There was already a demand, even at this early time, for plays in print.

The music at the king's court was the equal of any in the world. The king himself loved it. He used to sing to his own accompaniment on the harp, and there exists a song, 'Pastime with Good Company' which he himself composed. Whenever he went on a journey some of the choristers of the Chapel Royal went with him. The composers John Taverner and Thomas Tallis provided music for them. They were the founders of a great tradition of English church music which is one of the particular glories of the national culture.

In the sporting field also, with hawking and hunting, archery and jousting, King Henry led the way. No tournaments at the court of King Arthur could have been more magnificently presented than those which took place in the royal tilt-yards (see colour plate 3). Jousting was no longer simply a sporting exercise in hand-to-hand fighting, as it had once been, but had become a form of elaborate pageantry in its own right. The very suits of armour which the combatants wore were fantastically modelled and ornamented, with inlaid patterns of brass and gold upon them, unrivalled examples of the armourer's craft, fashioned for

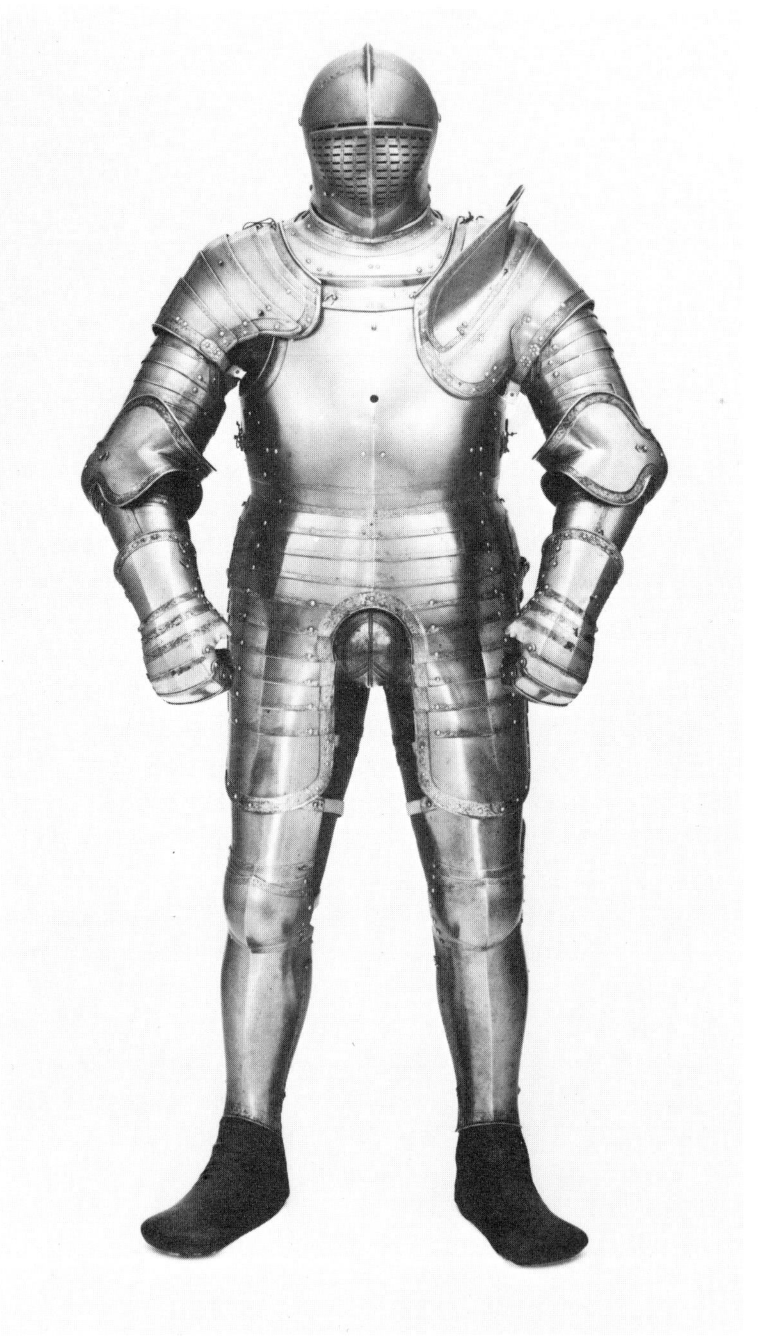

23. (a) Henry VIII's jousting armour.

(b) The armourer's skill: a fantastic helmet presented to Henry VIII by the Emperor Maximilian I.

the pageantry of romantic parades, not for the field of war. Examples of such armour, including King Henry's own suits (see plate 23), may be seen in the Tower of London.

The magnificence of the court was well matched by the splendour which attended the king's chief minister, Cardinal Wolsey. Throughout the first half of Henry VIII's reign the great Cardinal was in charge of all affairs of state, both at home and abroad. He behaved almost as though he were himself the king. At the same time he wisely made sure that the king was sufficiently satisfied in having his own way when he wanted it. That was essential. When in the end events came about in which the king could not be satisfied, and for which the Cardinal could not provide a remedy, the Cardinal fell from power, and matters suddenly took on a very different colour.

To restore the Golden Age of King Arthur was all very well, so far as it went, but of course it stopped some way short of the requirements of real life. King Arthur, in his imaginary Camelot, needed no successor. But for King Henry in his real kingdom, an heir to the throne was an urgent and real necessity; and that heir (the king was firmly convinced, and most people at the time would have agreed with him) had to be male. In this matter the king was frustrated. Queen Catherine of Aragon had given him one daughter only. All her other children had died at birth or in infancy. The king began to persuade himself that it had been a sin for him to have married his brother's widow – he found a text in the Book of Leviticus which confirmed it – and that his lack of a male heir was a punishment from Heaven. The pope who had allowed the marriage ought never to have done so. The king instructed Wolsey to approach the new pope, to make suitable arrangements for the marriage to be annulled.

Like a fuse to a powder-barrel, enormous political forces were at once touched off. The Emperor Charles V, who ruled Spain, the Netherlands, and half the rest of Europe, was Queen Catherine's nephew. He absolutely opposed any idea of divorce. The pope could not oppose the emperor. King Henry would not take no for an answer, even from the pope. Wolsey having failed the king, the king dismissed and disgraced him. Wolsey died soon after. The king, with the bit between his teeth, himself took over the government of the Church within his own country. He declared himself the head of it, and annexed all its property. The divorce was then proceeded with, and the king at once re-married. His new queen was a certain Anne Boleyn (see plate 24) a pretty lady of the court. In due course she gave birth to his baby. It was a girl.

King Henry endured his disappointment for a while, as best he could. The child was given the sumptuous christening that had been prepared in hopes of a boy. She was named Elizabeth. And still the king had no son to succeed him. In his vexation he was ready to listen to any sort of mischief. He heard rumours that Queen Anne Boleyn had behaved scandalously in the past, that even now she was unfaithful to him. She must go. Right or wrong, she was tried, found guilty, and beheaded.

We need not deal with the rest of the king's six marriages, and the events which, as he grew older, turned the would-be King

24. Anne Boleyn. Drawing by Hans Holbein.

Arthur into a sort of monstrous historical ogre. But it is ironical to note, in view of all his desperate shifts to produce an heir, that he is the only monarch on record who in fact produced three, each of whom succeeded him in turn.

The themes of history are always complex, and all simplifications, especially brief ones, should be treated with caution. It need hardly be said, therefore, that King Henry's break with the Church of Rome and his annexation of church property – the Dissolution of the Monasteries – was nothing like so simple, so sudden, or even so unexpected, as might appear from the brief account given here. It was all a part of the great European movement of the Reformation. In England the wealth and influence of the church and the clergy had for a long while been regarded with growing suspicion and hostility. The ostentatious power and wealth of Cardinal Wolsey by itself had been dangerous enough. It may be said that when King Henry seized and suppressed the monasteries he was only completing what his father had begun. Henry VII had revoked the powers of the mediaeval barons. Henry VIII was doing the same for the mediaeval church.

It is hard to believe that the King himself could have understood the magnitude of what he was doing. It is difficult, even today, looking back on it, to realize that King Henry's break with the Catholic Church, with all its consequences, was far and away the most significant event in English history since the Norman Conquest. It changed the whole social, political and cultural life of the country, almost at one stroke of the pen. No other event until the Industrial Revolution, not even the Civil War in Charles I's time, had such far-reaching political effect, or brought about so much social change.

It took place over a period of some fifteen years. The king's commissioners had to visit and report on every monastic foundation in the land. Opposition was regarded as treason, and punished accordingly. An armed uprising in the north, the Pilgrimage of Grace, was ferociously suppressed. But mostly the Dissolution took place in an orderly fashion, however sadly. Abbots and monks were turned out of their age-old homes. Lands and furniture were sold, frequently to a new class of landlording gentry, and the money went to help the king's Exchequer, which badly needed it. The monks and abbots and other clergy, however, were given pensions, those who had skills found other employment, and many took positions in the new state Church of England. Meanwhile the neighbouring yeomen and peasants looked around in the empty monasteries. Floors, doors, hinges and roof-tiles soon began to find themselves new homes.

We may wonder how ordinary people settled themselves down with the new manner of religion which the king had settled on them. Their whole observance of life and death had been altered by an act of law. The Arden family in Warwickshire, for example, had been brought up, generation after generation, with numerous monasteries in the country around them: Dominicans at Warwick and Kenilworth, Franciscans at Oxford, Benedictines at Coventry, and Cistercians at Hailes Abbey just over the Cotswolds. Now suddenly all these institutions, and all the things they stood for were demolished. At Hailes Abbey there had been a miraculous relic, the Holy Blood of Hailes, kept in a glass vessel set in silver. But now the king's commissioners had examined it and pronounced it nothing but the blood of a duck. What was one to think? And how was one to celebrate solemn family occasions? Thomas Arden was now a very old man; he could hardly be expected to change any ideas he might have about his funeral, at his time of life. His son Robert's wife had just given birth to another daughter, their eighth. With what ritual should the child now be christened? In fact she was christened, and named Mary, by the same parish priest and with the same ritual as all the others had been. And when old Thomas died his burial was conducted still in the traditional way, with the prayers in Latin. There were still a few years to pass before the first Book of Common Prayer, in English, began to be used in the churches. It was first issued in 1549.

But some years before that there had appeared on all the church lecterns in the land, by order of the king, the Great Bible printed in English from the translation of Miles Coverdale and others (see plate 25). The Bible in the common tongue was everywhere the cornerstone of Protestantism and the Reformation. The printing

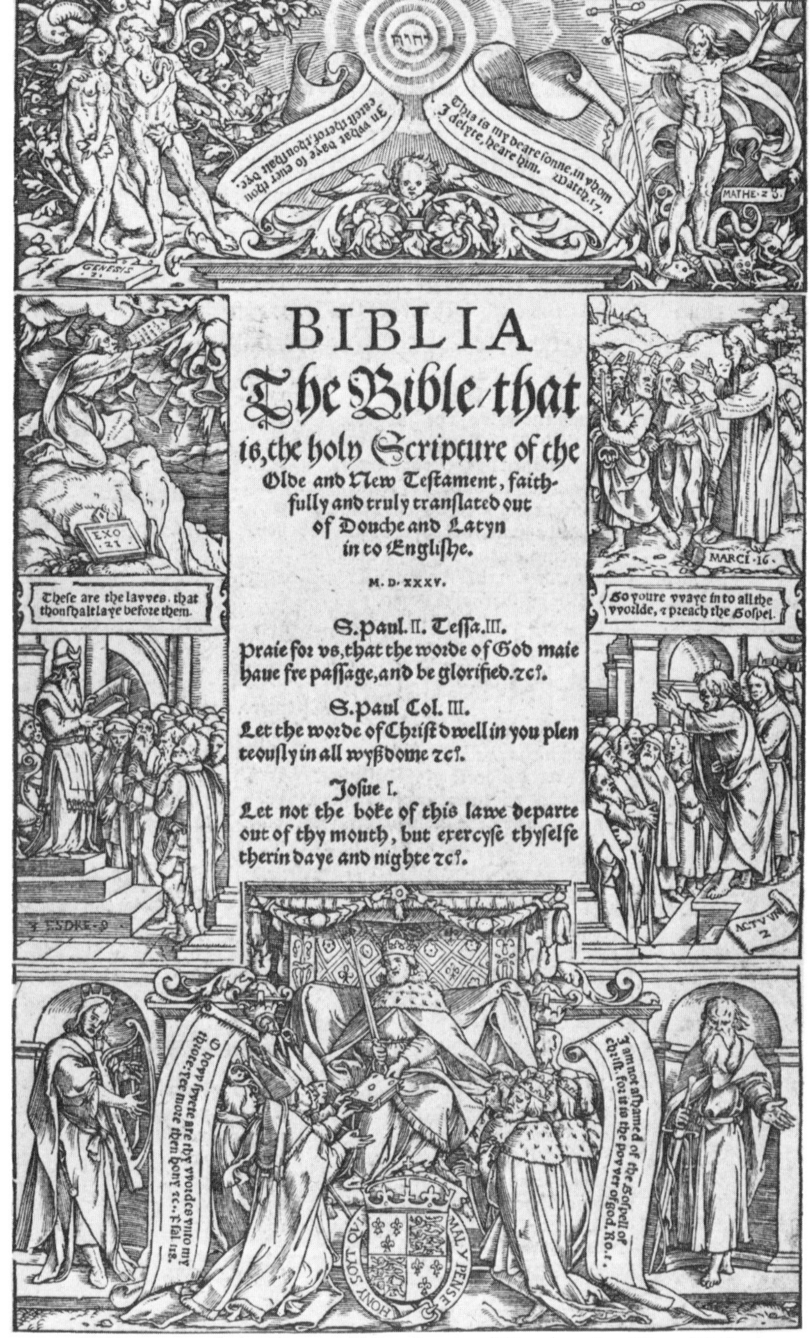

BIBLIA
The Bible/that
is, the holy Scripture of the
Olde and New Testament, faith-
fully and truly translated out
of Douche and Latyn
in to Englishe.

M. D. XXXV.

S. Paul. II. Tessa. III.
Praie for vs, that the worde of God maie
haue fre passage, and be glorified. &c.

S. Paul Col. III.
Let the worde of Christ dwell in you plen
teously in all wysdome &c.

Josue I.
Let not the boke of this lawe departe
out of thy mouth, but exercyse thyselfe
therin daye and nighte &c.

25. Title page of the Great Bible of 1535. Woodcut by Hans Holbein.

presses were the instruments which had made it quickly and widely available. Yet there were people still living in England at this time who as children might have seen William Caxton hang up his sign in the little side-street in Westminster, and peeped in at the door to watch the first English printers set to work.

THE REGIMENT OF WOMEN

As one approaches Hampton Court, the great brick-red palace built by Cardinal Wolsey in the days of his magnificence, one has the first impression of a castle (see plate 26). There one sees the towers, the battlements, the massive gateway, the wide moat with its bridge guarded on each side by heraldic beasts in stone, suitable for some legend of King Arthur out of Sir Thomas Malory's book. But of course it is not a castle. It is a nobleman's house, got up to look like one, on the principle that noblemen's houses ought somehow to look castle-like, with an air of power and of keeping people out. It is, so to speak, a castle that has been tamed. The days of the real, warlike castles were over.

It is possible to imagine that the old castles had been tamed and domesticated, in the end, by the ladies who had planted their rose-gardens on the battlements. Like home-making and housekeeping and all such other civilizing things, gardening had usually been considered a matter for women. Her garden was part of a housewife's economy. She cultivated her fruit bushes, her kitchen vegetables, her medicinal herbs (for she was the family pharmacist), her sweet-smelling herbs for the linen-press or for strewing the floors, and flowers, especially for their perfume, which she distilled. It all went in with her busy domestic day. Beyond that she did not usually seek to go. That 'a woman's place is in the home' was a teaching easier to accept in days when women had little time or opportunity to be anywhere else. From that it was only a short step to thinking that it was actually not *natural* for women to be elsewhere, or to want to be.

26. The towered gateway to Hampton Court Palace. A Tudor 'castle' in brick.

A lady enclosed in a fair walled garden, with music and fountains and flowers around her, where the bold fighting man from the harsh world outside might visit her for solace and comfort on his days off, was, we recall, a notion much cultivated in the Middle Ages. Even so, it carried with it the idea that the bold fighting man would be weakened for the strenuous business of life outside if he allowed himself to dally too long in the enchantments of the garden. He would be ensnared, as Samson was by Delilah. By the same token, women with their soft weakening influences should not be allowed to meddle in men's affairs. They could not hope to manage them properly, and should not try. So even when women had time and opportunity to take part in things other than domestic affairs – in business or government, for example – they usually did not do so. Those who, in spite of everything, found or put themselves in positions of political power, could be regarded as unnatural, if not actually diabolical, like the ferocious Queen Margaret of Anjou in the Wars of the Roses, or Joan of Arc, who was burned as a witch.

It was in the time of the Tudors that women at last began to come out from the shadow of all that ancient nonsense. By an accident of history in the middle of the sixteenth century the kingdom of England came in turn under the rule of two women, Mary Tudor (see plate 27) and her half-sister Elizabeth; the kingdom of Scotland, of Mary of Lorraine, and her daughter Mary Queen of Scots; while the effective ruler of France for half a century was the formidable queen-mother Catherine de'Medici. Confronted by this appalling rebellion against nature (for so he considered it) the Scottish Protestant leader John Knox wrote and published a frantic sermon against it, which he called *A First Blast of the Trumpet Against the Monstrous Regiment of Women.* Even after we have reminded ourselves that words have changed their meanings – 'monstrous regiment' meant simply 'unnatural rule' – the title's militant suggestion of women on the march, though rather before its time in a general sense, is not unsuitable. John Knox had the misfortune to publish his attack in the year Queen Elizabeth came to the English throne and she did not forgive him for it. She reigned for forty-five years, and proved him wrong in every one of them.

Away in Warwickshire, in the family home in Wilmcote, Robert Arden had female problems of his own to contend with. He had his eight daughters to bring up and find suitable husbands for, not to mention finding dowries for them. Their mother was dead and he had recently married again, to a widow who was a much needed help for the family in those difficult days. For difficult they were: the news from Warwick and Stratford was that the old king had died. His son, now King Edward VI (see plate 28), was still only a boy. It was learned there was a new Earl of Warwick (but nobody locally had heard of him: he was not one of the old family) who had become the king's chief minister. Protector Somerset, the former minister, had been beheaded for some treachery or other. Then it was heard that the new Earl of Warwick had been created Duke of Northumberland, and then that he, too, had been beheaded for some other treachery, following the sickness and death of the young king (after only six years on the throne) and the accession of his half-sister, the new Queen Mary. What next?

27. Queen Mary. Painting by Antonis Mor, 1554.

Queen Mary was a Catholic, and the talk was that she was about to restore the old religion. Robert had probably never forsaken the old one so far as observances went, so that in itself did not much disturb him; but he and many of his friends had bought church land when the monasteries were sold up, and the fear was that the queen's commissioners might come and take it all back again. It was also learned that she intended to marry the Crown Prince Philip of Spain. Then it was confirmed that she had done so, in Winchester Cathedral, and that London was full of Spaniards and monks. The queen was, after all, half Spanish herself, being Catherine of Aragon's daughter. Then there was news of cruelty and persecution, of Protestant bishops burned alive for their faith, of confessions under torture, of rebellions and reprisals, of martyrdoms and hatred. Country people shut their doors and hoped the storm would not blow their way. It was trouble enough that money was worth only half its old value nowadays, that the continuing enclosing of lands by the landlords (Robert Arden for one) was throwing more and more labourers out of work, who joined with gangs of other 'masterless men', so that the highways were becoming increasingly dangerous after dark, because of their maraudings.

But most of these troubles lay beyond the Warwickshire horizon. Robert's way of life went on much as before. He grew older, and actually continued to prosper. He added to his estates in Wilmcote and Snitterfield. Five of his eight daughters were married by now, and one of his tenants in Snitterfield had a son who seemed very interested in Mary, his youngest. This young man, John Shakespeare, seemed pleasant and resourceful. He was just out of his apprenticeship, and talked of setting up in the soft-leather business in Stratford. Mary seemed to favour him. Henry Field, the Stratford tanner, a friend of the Arden family, had a good opinion of him, and might be expected to put business his way. It was perhaps a pity that Shakespeare was such a common name. There had been a Fellow called Shakespeare at Merton College, Oxford, not many years before, who had thought the name so much beneath his dignity that he had had it changed to Saunders. But after all, what's in a name? A husband was a hus-

28. King Edward VI, c. 1546.

band. Robert had ruefully to consider that, having no son, the family name of which he was so proud would die with him. Shakespeare as a name, however common, was better than nothing.

Robert died in 1556. From the way his will was worded it has been thought he died a Catholic. It should be remembered that the Catholic Queen Mary was still on the throne and Catholic observances were demanded by law. People like Robert Arden could not be expected to be changing their religious practices with every change of reign. Meanwhile in his will he left an estate of fifty acres to his daughter Mary. John Shakespeare married her soon after. He had married an heiress, and he had bought his own house and shop in Stratford. He was on his way up in the world.

SCHOOLDAYS

WHEN Henry VIII suppressed the monasteries and confiscated their property, one of the results – an accidental casualty of the event – was the breakdown of a system of education that had existed in England for over four hundred years. Schools for teaching 'grammar' (a word which in earlier times meant more than it does today: it had to do with the art of clear thinking, as well as of the construction of language) had been set up in the greater churches of the Christian world, by order of the pope, as far back as the days of William the Conqueror. From this, in time, there had developed a universal network of education based upon a universal language: Latin. Latin, indeed, was the principal study at these schools. It was supposed to lead to the possession of an articulate and disciplined mind, with a language which could serve you wherever in the world you found yourself; and so, in a large measure it did. By the end of the Middle Ages the system had created a civilization that was far more literate, and spread over a far wider range of the social order than is sometimes believed. As evidence of this, as soon as the first printing-presses were set up, there was an immediate demand for all the books they could print. There was already a literate public waiting for them. When in England the appetite for books proved greater than Caxton and his successors could at first satisfy, the London grocers, with a ready eye to the market, imported books from the printing houses in the Netherlands, and sold them along with their currants and spices.

It was the loss of money, not simply the closing of the monastery buildings, which starved and halted the church-run schools for nearly a generation. For, besides the wealth of the monasteries themselves, there had been great endowments bequeathed to the church by rich people to pay for prayers to be said, in perpetuity, for their souls in the next world, and for the maintenance of schools, as a pious contribution to this one. But the king's commissioners now declared that the prayer money was being spent on a needless superstition, and requisitioned it for the royal purse; and as often as not the school money somehow went along with the prayer-money.

The king at this time was no longer the old Henry, but his son Edward VI, who was still only a child. A council of ministers therefore did the work for him (and made a good profit from it for themselves) and the king did as he was told. Not all the schools were closed. Those that were spared, separated from the old church management, became known as 'Edward VI Grammar Schools'. Many of these are still in existence, proudly retaining that old title. In time money was restored for the re-opening of other schools under the management or supervision of local town councils. The grammar school at Stratford-upon-Avon (see plate 29) was one of these. Its endowments were restored for the education of the sons of burgesses of the town, in 1553, the last year of the young king's reign.

In principle, the education of the sons of citizens, wherever there was a grammar school available, was free, though wealthier people were expected to pay a contribution. Then as now, education was considered a rightful and necessary inheritance for all boys. But not, in those days, for all girls. The foreseeable future lives of girls were not likely to require the sort of education boys would need. They had all their many domestic duties to be trained in, which were difficult and tiresome enough on their own, without the added confusion of overburdening their brains.

It was different, however, for the children of gentle or noble birth. These were educated at home, usually by private tutors, the girls as well as the boys. Girls of high rank did not usually show a very determined enthusiasm for household chores, and were

29. The Grammar School at Stratford-upon-Avon. The old schoolroom as it is today.

certainly never expected to do any; so there was nothing for it, to keep them from the sin of idleness, but to allow them to be educated – even to insist upon it. From this it soon became evident enough that women could be every inch as good scholars as men, and often better. Queen Elizabeth was herself an outstanding example. She knew her Latin as well as any man, could listen to long speeches in it and reply to them in kind, and quote her classical authors with the best.

The absolute dominance of Latin as the central instrument of a civilized education was in Tudor times, as before, never for a moment in question. In the centuries that followed, it did very slowly decline from its majestic importance; but only within living memory has it actually ceased to be taught in a majority of schools, except as a specialist subject. In the Tudor grammar schools it flattened nearly all other subjects out of existence with the ponderousness of a road-roller. For a younggentleman being educated at home, however, things could be more liberal and interesting. It was assumed he would have to go out into the world among people of wide experience and culture, and so would need to have a good grounding in accomplishments of which the grammar school boy might only pick up a smattering as an optional extra in his senior years if he was lucky, or out of school hours if he had the chance. These 'extra' subjects included history, geography, music and modern languages. Of course the private scholar had to learn his Latin as well as the rest, but the liberality and wider range of his education did of itself tend to form a class-distinction between the gentleman's son and the tradesman's son.

A boy usually went to his grammar school at the age of seven. Before that, when he was about five, he would have gone to a 'petty-school', where he would have been taught to read and write. He learned his first principles from a horn book, which was a sheet of paper or vellum, printed with the alphabet and a few simple combinations of vowels and consonants, mounted on a little board with a handle to it, protected by a sheet of transparent horn. The petty schools were kept by poor people, usually elderly dames, as a means of scraping a living, and we are told they did not make very good teachers. One writer at the time described them as 'men or women altogether rude, and altogether ignorant of the due composing and just spelling of words'; so perhaps it is not surprising that he went on to complain that there were too many boys of seven or eight 'that can neither readily spell or rightly write even the common words of our English'. However that might have been, at seven or eight off they went to the grammar school and the Latin.

The grammar school day began at seven in the morning in winter time; in summer at six. The children worked till nine, when there would be an 'intermission' for them to eat the breakfast they had brought with them, and prepare the next lesson, and perhaps even play, if there was time. Much time there could not have been, because the intermission didn't last much beyond a quarter of an hour, after which it was back to work till eleven.

Then the boys would go off home for their dinner, which was the principal meal of the day. By one o'clock they were back at school again, to work on till five or half-past. Once a week they had a half-holiday, which began at three in the afternoon. It was called a 'remedy'. Besides this there were the public holidays of the church year, such as Corpus Christi; and there were vacations, eighteen days at Christmas, twelve at Easter, and a week at Whitsuntide.

Discipline in Tudor schools was harsh (see plate 30). How else could a few rigid-minded teachers, with such a heavy-going programme, quell and control large classes of growing boys, except by the rod? Besides, it was the common belief about all children at that time, that they are by nature rebellious, that is to say sinful; and therefore they must be brought into submission by any possible means. Spare the rod and spoil the child. A schoolmaster must be master in fact and deed. He hung up his birch-rod on the wall behind his chair, where all the school might see it, and he used it vigorously in sight of all the school upon any rebellious

30. A schoolmaster with his pupils. Woodcut from a handbook on education (note the cane on the table)

occasion. Not to have learned one's lesson properly counted as a rebellion in itself.

Was it as bad as it sounds? (see plate 31). There were some enlightened and humane teachers, like Roger Ascham, tutor to Princess Elizabeth, who was horrified at the brutality of the floggings in the schools, saying that as a result boys 'carry commonly from school with them a hatred of their master and a continual contempt for learning'. And there was Richard Mulcaster, headmaster of Merchant Taylors School, whose ideas in favour of a more liberal and varied education, for the simple purpose of making it actually *interesting* for children, and especially of the equal value of the English language along with Latin, were so far in advance of their time that they were not appreciated or followed until more than two hundred years after his death. Besides, if a system is to be judged by its fruits, the Tudor schools must be allowed at least a little of the credit for an age which produced some of the most remarkable men and women in English history.

Good schools are made by good teachers, and in the middle of the Tudor century, as more and more schools began to be founded or re-opened, after their closing with the monasteries, it might have been difficult to find enough teachers to run them;

31. The 'petty school' in an industrious and good-humoured mood. Detail from a drawing by Pieter-Breughel.

but, fortunately, just at this time the greatest of all teaching aids was beginning to find its way, first onto the schoolmaster's table, and soon, as its numbers rapidly increased, into the schoolboy's satchel; the cheaply produced printed school-book. No longer was it necessary to memorize every phrase of a lesson by repeating it parrot-fashion after the master. If one had to memorize (as one had) one could now do it out of the book, which was likely to be better as well as easier. Every schoolboy's primer, which he began to memorize as soon as he entered the grammar school, was William Lily's *Grammatica Latina*, which must have been one of the world's first best-sellers, as in Elizabethan times it is estimated to have sold 10,000 copies a year, a very great number indeed for those days. Then there was a book of Latin maxims, also to be learned by heart; and there were *Aesop's Fables*. Ahead, in the higher grades, were Ovid's *Metamorphoses*, and Caesar's *Gallic War* and Livy's *History of Rome*; and so on to the plays of Terence and Plautus and Seneca, which the senior boys might even learn to act. Here they all were, printed and bound in little books, held in the boy's own hand.

It may be useful to pause here, and imagine a boy with a book in his hand, at Stratford grammar school in the year 1571. He is ten years old, and his name is Richard Field. He is the son of Henry Field the Stratford tanner. His book is a copy of Ovid, brand new, just arrived at the school. He opens it carefully, examines the fresh new pages, still smelling faintly of the printer's ink. He examines the binding, wishing (let us suppose) that it were leather, not plain vellum. His father sometimes tans and dyes fine leathers for the bookbinding trade. His father's friend and colleague, Master Shakespeare the alderman, with his prosperous glove and leather-goods business in Henley Street has customers for it at the bindery in Oxford. Richard has seen printers and binders at work there. He thinks he himself would rather become a printer than follow his father's trade as a tanner. Tanning is a stinking, filthy work. Printing is for gentlmen and scholars. But alas, now he is caught day-dreaming. The master bangs down the rod on the table in front of him. Richard Field, stand up at once and decline the present tense of *studere*, to be eager or diligent, to study.

CHURCH AND STATE

HENRY VIII had had the English Bible placed on the lectern in every English church. Edward VI had had the English Book of Common Prayer placed alongside. But the book which Queen Mary's reign brought forth was of a different order, of her doing certainly, but certainly not of her choosing. John Foxe's *Acts and Monuments of These Latter and Perilous Times* was printed in 1563, five years after her death. It is an account of the burnings, killings and dreadful sufferings of those who had refused to submit to her passionate determination to lead the people back into the old way of religion, her mother Catherine's religion, which her father had rejected. Foxe's *Book of Martyrs* (as it is usually called) was now likewise placed in the churches beside the Bible and the Prayer Book. Extracts from it were read aloud during the service, and it was a powerful influence in confirming the minds of English people against any further thought of returning to the old faith (see plate 32).

Queen Mary herself was a bitter and tragic person. She was unwise in her actions and doomed to disappointment in their results. Her marriage to Philip of Spain was perhaps her greatest personal disappointment. He and his following of Spanish courtiers were hated in England wherever they went. His priests were believed to be the queen's advisers and teachers in the burning of her Protestant bishops. He himself was politely disdainful and unkind. There were no children of the marriage. He had already returned to Spain, and was finding continual reasons for staying

32. The burning of the Protestant bishops, Latymer and Ridley. Woodcut from Foxe's *Book of Martyrs*.

there, away from her, when Queen Mary died, after only a five years' reign. English people were glad to be rid of both of them. Having said which, it is necessary to add that nobody in later times has written about her without noting the personal good qualities she certainly possessed, and regretting the waste of her unhappy life.

So her sister Elizabeth came to the throne amid acclamations of rejoicing, thankfulness and hope for the future (see colour plate 4). The hope was never disappointed; yet it might well have been thought, because of the dangers and cruelties that had surrounded her childhood and the obvious dangers that lay ahead, that there could not have been much ground for hope in her. The night before her coronation she lodged in the Tower of London attended by all the ceremonious comforts belonging to a queen. Yet, not so very long before, she had been there under lock and key, her sister's prisoner, suspected of being a centre for conspiracy and treason; and from the battlement walk where she used to take her daily exercise she could see into the yard where the scaffold stood, where her mother Anne Boleyn had knelt down to be beheaded, at her father's orders. Since her father's death there had been nothing but insurrections, treacheries, executions, burnings, defiance, and the kingdom in peril, as if instead of King Arthur and the golden age, it was the bad old days of the Wars of the Roses that had returned. Such a possibility still lay ahead of her as she set forth from the Tower in the morning of Sunday January 15th, 1550, through the City of London towards Westminster Abbey. To the speeches of welcome given her by the Lord Mayor and aldermen of the City she replied: 'I will be as good unto you as ever Queen was to her people. And for the safety and quietness of you all I will not spare, if need be, to spend my blood.' She was then twenty-five years old.

Henry VIII's religious revolution had not in fact greatly divided the nation, because it was in step with feelings that were already very general in the country; and he was most careful, in the changes he made in the services and rituals of the church, not to change them very much. Sudden changes in the ownership of property (as in the case of the monasteries) was one thing: but radical changes in what people were supposed to believe was quite another. Queen Mary's mistake had been to try to put the clock back, to force people to return to a belief they had been of two minds about in the first instance.

Queen Elizabeth followed her father's plan. Throughout her long reign she contrived to establish the Church of England as a careful balance between the Church of Rome, with its ritualized forms of worship, and the plainer practices of the Protestant Reformation. As a result the more extreme English Protestants were just as much against the middle-of-the-road Church of England as the Catholics were, if not more so. They saw it as a compromise with idolatry on the road to damnation. The Church of England, they declared, ought to be 'purified' from any taint of such 'Romish' practices. Thus they began to be known as 'puritans'.

Puritanism was in its own way a new social culture arising among a newly educated sort of people, who were later to be called 'middle class' (though that term was not then known). It was based upon personal reading of the Bible, which had now been made easily available, by the printing press, for private study by individual men and women. It appealed to their individual consciences before God, not to the great establishments of the State. 'In all things we must first look what is the Lord's will . . . and then what is the will of man', wrote Robert Browne, one of the most influential of Elizabethan puritans. Such men preached to eager listeners and wrote for eager readers. Their sermons, tracts and pamphlets came from the printing-presses by the hundred score.

But ifevery man, woman, family or group may find the Word of God for themselves and interpret it in their own way, a state religion will then be open to conflicting interpretations from every side, and break up into fragments, with the followers of different doctrines quarrelling among themselves. This was what the church establishment in Elizabeth's reign was determined to avoid. Fortunately the majority of people were themselves glad to follow the middle way, and willing to be shown what it was. Even so, it was thought wise to assist them in forming the habit, and so it was enacted as law that all the queen's subjects, including children over the age of six, must attend both the morning and afternoon services at their parish church every Sunday and feast day. It was the business of the churchwardens to keep an eye on parishioners, and the head of every household was responsible for his family's attendance. If there were too many absences without excuse, he would have a fine to pay. Local puritans, though they might think it their duty to grumble out loud during the service, had nevertheless to put in their attendances. The same applied to such Catholics as might be: those who privately kept to their old faith prudently kept it to themselves. And after all, there were still very many older people around who had been brought up as Catholics, before the old king changed it all. John Shakespeare and his wife Mary – Mary Arden that was – were both still young people when Elizabeth was crowned, yet they could well remember the Catholic habits of their own parents.

Church services were long. The morning service began at seven with a Psalm. Then came the Lessons from the Old and New Testament, the Litany, the Communion, a sermon or homily from the pulpit, which would go on for a considerable while, and then more psalms. A baptism of infants would follow. The afternoon service began at two, and would include another sermon and an hour's catechism for young people. Schoolboys next day would be required by their master to give a full account of the sermon, together with its text.

That might be all very well in the summer, but in winter time, in a bitterly cold church one must hope that the parson tempered the wind a little to his parishioners. One of these parishioners, Mary Shakespeare's son William, has left us what could be a recollection of the trudge through the streets, three quarters of a mile, from their Stratford home in Henley Street to the parish church, through the mud, 'when blood is nipped and ways be foul', sitting there on a cold bench, everybody huddled together for warmth, trying to catch the text, 'when all aloud the wind doth blow' outside the church windows, 'and coughing drowns the parson's saw' from the pulpit. William is only eight, a junior boy at the grammar school. Not far off one of the older boys, Richard Field, the tanner's son, seems to have borrowed some older and bigger person's shoes, and stuffed them with straw to keep his feet warm. That might be worth remembering next Sunday.

SPORTS AND PAGEANTS

'... THEY bedeck themselves with scarfs, ribbons and laces hanged all over with gold rings, precious stones and other jewels: this done, they tie about their legs twenty or forty bells, with rich handkerchiefs in their hands ... borrowed for the most part of their pretty Mopsies and loving Bessies, for bussing* them in the dark. Thus all things set in order, they have their hobby-horses, dragons and other antics, together with their bawdy pipers and thundering drummers to strike up the devils dance withal ... and in this sort they go to church (I say) and into the church (though the minister be at prayer or preaching) dancing and swinging their handkerchiefs over their heads in the church like devils incarnate ...'

Thus, with much more of the same sort, in tones of shocked indignation, wrote the puritan preacher Philip Stubbes. He was describing the festive arrival, at Christmas, of the Lord of Misrule and his followers. The idea of setting up somebody as a Lord of Misrule seems to have begun in ancient times, when the Roman soldiers and their families in Britain celebrated their winter feast the Saturnalia. The handkerchiefs, bells and ribbons which Stubbes refers to are features of Morris dancing (see plate 33) which was everywhere very popular in Tudor England. The word 'Morris' is a corruption of 'Moorish'. It originated with a dance brought over from Moorish Spain in the days of Edward III. The hobby-horses and dragons (see plate 34 and colour plate 5) may

* Kissing.

33. Will Kempe, a famous Morris dancer, with his piper Tom Shy. Woodcut from his *Nine Day's Wonder*, an account of how he danced from London to Norwich.

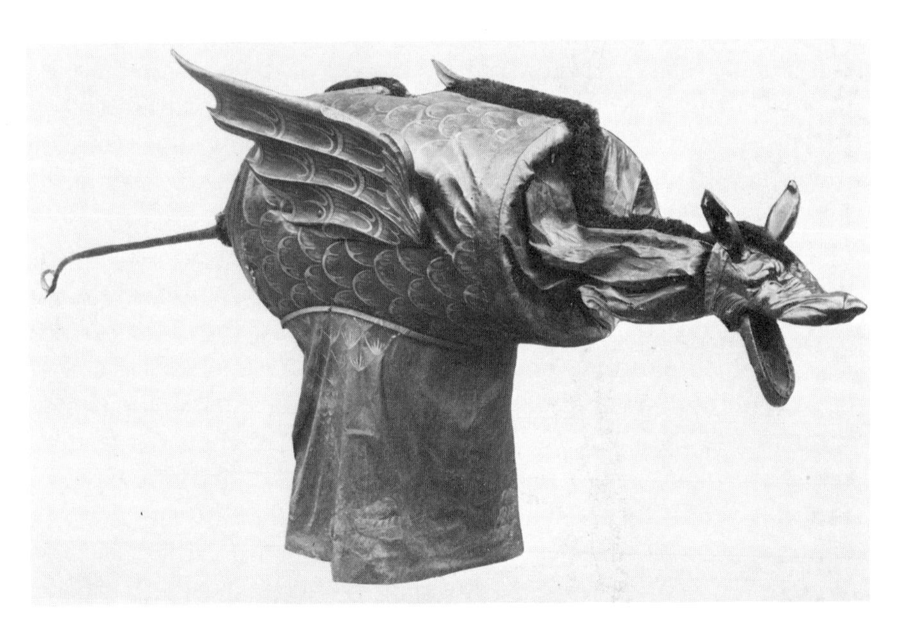

34. Snap the dragon, a festival figure from Tudor times, once familiar in the streets of Norwich. The wearer's legs are hidden by the skirt. The head is moved on a pole, the jaws with a string.

be found going round the streets at festival times in a few English country towns, such as Minehead in Somerset, and Padstow in Cornwall, even today.

Another game which, it is thought, the Romans brought with them was football. In Tudor times it was a very simple kick-about game played at festival times such as Shrove Tuesday, by as many players as liked to join in (two or three hundred, for example) over as much ground as might lie between one village and the next. The ball was an inflated bladder protected by a leather casing sewn together by the local cobbler. As to the game itself, listen once more to Philip Stubbes in his shocked, pulpit matter:

'As concerning football, I protest unto you it may rather be called a friendly kind of fight, than a play or recreation; a bloody and murdering practice, than a fellowly sport or pastime. For doth not every one lie in wait for his adversary, seeking to overthrow him and pitch him on his nose, though it be upon hard stones, in ditch or dale, in valley or hill, or what place soever it be he careth not, so he have him down . . . So by this means sometimes their necks are broken, sometimes their backs, sometimes their legs, sometimes their arms, sometime one part thrust out of joint, sometime another, sometime their noses gush out with blood, sometime their eyes start out, and sometimes hurt in one place, sometimes in another.'

In spite of which, somehow the sport survived.

What made the pious Stubbes complain so violently was not so much the sports themselves (his descriptions are enriched with a certain relish) but the fact they took place on church festivals and Holy Days. It might perhaps have been allowable, in his view, if they had taken place at any other time. But there were no other times: these were the only holidays people had. So, after morning church, families had the rest of the day for recreation, and made the most of it.

There were no organized games as we understand them. Recreation mostly took the form of exercises in physical or warlike skills, running and wrestling, fighting at quarterstaff and, above all, archery. The skill of the English longbowmen, like the exploits of their folk-hero Robin Hood, was a potent legend inherited from the Middle Ages, and was strongly encouraged by all the Tudor monarchs, especially Henry VIII, who was an excellent archer himself. In Tudor times archers were called 'artillery', and had their place on the battlefield alongside guns and muskets. So, on holiday afternoons, the citizens of the archery guilds would stand to their practice in the fields outside the towns and villages all over the country, not always without some danger to passers-by. A little girl playing with her friends in Moorfields, which in those days was an open common outside the northern wall of London, a well-known ground for archery practice, ran home one afternoon with an arrow through her hat. Later in life, after she had become a wealthy woman, she founded a school for girls as a thank-offering for her escape.

The way in which public festivals are carried on from age to age in spite of political or other changes which, one might suppose, should have brought them to an end, may well be seen in the continuance during nearly the whole of the Tudor period of the famous mediaeval Mystery Plays which were still given every June on the feast of Corpus Christi, as they had been given for four hundred years, in the towns of York, Lincoln, Chester, Wakefield and Coventry. These were the most famous of the many festivals of their kind, and many of their scenes were written down, and so preserved for us, in the middle of the sixteenth century; but there had been others, now long forgotten. Coventry is not very far from Stratford-on-Avon, and it is reasonable to think that at some time, say in the year 1571, when he had become Chief Alderman of Stratford and a justice of the Peace, that a distinguished citizen such as John Shakespeare would have gone there, perhaps as an official visitor, to witness these famous plays, taking his family with him. His eldest son William was then just beginning at the grammar school.

A 'mystery' was a trade or skill, and the Mystery Plays were so called because each of the trade guilds of the town was responsible for its own play, part of a long sequence of plays which, together, told the whole Bible story from Adam and Eve to the crucifixion of Christ and the Last Judgement. Each episode was performed upon a 'pageant', which was a high stage mounted on wheels, suitably dressed up to represent the scene of its episode, the Garden of Eden, Noah's Ark, Herod's Palace, or whatever it might be. The episodes were distributed among the various Guilds in an appropriate way: thus, the carpenters and masons would deal with the Building of the Temple; the goldsmiths, by long tradition, would enact the coming of the Three Kings with their precious gifts of gold, frankincense and myrrh; the fish-mongers anything to do with St Peter (because he was a fisher-man); and every year the dreadful butchers would be responsible for the crucifixion. The audiences for these plays would gather at pre-arranged station-places around the town, and all day long from early morning till evening the procession of pageants would roll by, from one station to the next, playing their famous scenes over and over again. The guildsmen actors were doubtless proud of their skill, and would often hand on their parts, in their own families from one generation to the next.

But the pageant plays were a passing show in these later times, in more senses than one. In their heyday they had been a means of making people familiar with the unfolding story told in the Bible; but now that more and more people could read, and some even had Bibles of their own, there was less and less need for this. Besides which, religious festivals of this kind were too closely linked with Catholic practices to be wholly approved by the Church of England and its clergy; and the everyday vulgarities in which some of the scenes from the sacred Book were often acted gravely offended people like the puritan Parson Stubbes and his fellows. And lastly, the amateur actors, good as they may have been in their way, no longer had the field to themselves. Their towns were now being visited more and more often by little companies of professionals.

From a respectable citizen's point of view, acting could hardly rank as a profession in any proper sense. Who were these men who did it, after all? Did they not tramp the roads from town to town? Were they not therefore vagabonds? But no, the members of this young profession had taken care to protect themselves against any such dangerous imputation which might have landed them in the lock-up as 'sturdy beggars' or 'masterless men', and turned them off with a flogging. A company of professional actors had to enrol itself under the protection of some nobleman or other, as his 'servants'. They could then wear his livery (which he provided) and travel the roads with his badge on their cart (see plate 35). They would come to town as My Lord Rich's Men, or The Earl of Oxford's Men, or whoever it might be. The actors were an odd lot, but they had standing.

During his year of office as High Bailiff of Stratford, John Shakespeare welcomed two well-known companies to his town, the Queen's Men, and the Earl of Worcester's. Their first performances would, according to custom, be given before him and an invited audience in the Guild Hall, for which he himself would pay them. After that they would give public performances at one of the local inns, usually in the afternoons, on a stage set up in the yard, and collect their money in pennies at the gate. Stratford became a favourite stopping place for actors' companies in the

35. Travelling players approaching a city. (Modern drawing.)

years following. The inns where they played were all hardly more than a stone's throw from the Shakespeares' house in Henley Street, hardly more than a step aside on a boy's way home from school of a summer's evening. If the afternoon's performance was finished one might still perhaps have a glimpse of the actors packing up, over there by the stage, even perhaps have a word with one of them.

One of the companies that played at Stratford from time to time was The Earl of Leicester's Men. The earl's castle being at Kenilworth, only twelve miles away, perhaps it is not surprising that they should often be in the neighbourhood, for they would be called, upon occasion, to entertain their patron and his guests when he was in residence. One very great occasion was in 1575, when the queen herself was his guest. Robert Dudley, Earl of Leicester, whom the queen loved but would not marry, (though most of her people, certainly not excluding the Earl himself, hoped she would) had spared no expense in money and imagination to make her three weeks' stay at his castle an event so romantically conceived and carried out that it was described in full by one who was there, under the title of 'The Princely Pleasures of Kenilworth'. Some at least of the earl's players must have been present to play their parts in the fantastic diversions which took place every day. At the queen's first arrival she was intercepted at the gate by a monstrous Porter with a huge club and keys, who grumbled away at all the inexplicable fuss and excitement that was disturbing his rest, until he understood the cause of it. Then he was tamed and shamed, and knelt and handed over his keys to the queen. Upon the battlements over the gate were six figures of gigantic trumpeters, eight feet high, who then lifted their enormous trumpets and sounded a fanfare (though the real sounding was done by real trumpeters hidden behind). 'And by this show' says the account 'it was meant that in the days and reign of King Arthur men were of that stature; so that the Castle of Kenilworth should be seen still to be kept by Arthur's heirs.' The theme of King Arthur, and the earl's claim to be descended from him, was several times brought in thereafter. That evening the Lady of the Lake 'upon a moveable island, bright blazing with torches', came floating across the castle lake to where the queen stood on an ornamental bridge, specially built for the occasion. The Lady told how she had been mistress of the enchanted lake ever since King Arthur's time, but now she was surrendering her charge to the queen. In another episode a few days later the Lady of the Lake appeared again on her floating island, accompanied by Arion riding and singing on the back of a dolphin. 'The dolphin', says the record, 'was conveyed upon a boate, so that the owers seemed to be his fynnes'. It was twenty-four feet long from head to tail, and in it were hidden

36. A royal entertainment on the water, with a great artificial sea-creature, as at Kenilworth in 1575. (French tapestry, c. 1573.)

six musicians 'casting sound from the dolphin's belly within; Arion, the seventh, sitting thus singing (as I say) without' (see plate 36).

On many days the queen and the earl went out 'hunting at force', that is hunting the stag with hounds. The art, methods and ceremonial courtesies of this pastime, (which was still chiefly reserved for royalty and the nobility over their own lands and deer-parks) are all fully described in the *Booke of Hunting* by one Francis Turberville, printed at about this time. Turberville, in another book, *The Booke of Falconrie*, has a picture showing the queen and her gentlemen out hawking, with her hawk 'stooping' to bring down a heron (see plate 37). The earl kept the queen's

37. Queen Elizabeth out hawking with her gentlemen.

own pack of stag-hounds at Kenilworth. While the royal party were taking their refreshment in the woods at the end of the day they would be entertained by a speech from a Savage Man clad all in moss and ivies, who would appear from among the trees; or perhaps with a little play of Diana and her nymphs; or by Sylvanus the forest god with his story of an enchanted Holly Bush, and jolly woodland jokes about a He-Holly and a She-Holly. And on other days, at the castle, there would be entertainments in the tournament yard. One of these had a rustic theme, a village wedding or 'bride-ale', a knock-about burlesque with clowns and fools and morris-dancers; and this was followed by a comic play performed 'by certain good-harted men of Coventree'.

And then of an evening the queen would walk in the earl's private garden under the battlements, 'wherein hard along the castle wall is reared a pleasant terrace . . . even under foot, and fresh of fine grass'. The garden below was 'much gracified by due proportion of four even quarters'. It had arbours, and obelisks and pyramids of porphyry, topped by orbs and spheres, and there was (as described in his own spelling by an eye-witness, one Robert Laneham) 'sweetness of savour on all sides, made so respiraunt from the redolent plants and fragrant earbs and floourz, in foorm, cooler, and quantitee so deliciously variant; and frute trees bedecked with applz, peares, and ripe cherryez.'

Nevertheless when the lady of the battlement garden set out again on her royal progress, homewards to her own palaces at Richmond or Nonesuch, the earl was still no nearer knowing whether or not she would marry him. We know now that she never did.

All along the rutted roads the people from the nearby towns and villages were lining the way to watch her procession pass by. All the time she was at Kenilworth they had come every day to the castle gate to see her on her way out hunting, or see the shows on the lake from across the water, or the wonderful fireworks of an evening. It was certainly worth a twelve-mile walk from Stratford. It would have been strange if the grammar school master had not given his boys at least one day off to go and see the queen. William Shakespeare was then eleven years old.

SHIPS AND SPANIARDS

THERE were old people still alive in the 1570s who, as children, might have watched Catherine of Aragon pass by on her royal progress to London to be married to Prince Arthur. We must recall that when Catherine herself was a child at the court of Ferdinand and Isabella, she had witnessed the triumphal welcome given by them to Christopher Columbus, on his return from his first voyage of discovery to America. In the space of one lifetime since then, the whole planetary world had been unfolded. The oceans around it had ceased to be mysterious barriers, but had become open roadways for any ships well enough built and equipped to travel them. Gone, now, except for pottering along friendly coastlines, were the sort of tubby carracks and caravels Columbus had used, and which had carried the princess Catherine and her company to England. A generation later, when Philip of Spain made the same journey to marry Mary Tudor, he came with a squadron of galleons, a new type of ocean-going warship, which may have been calculated to impress the English by their great gun-lined hulls and spread of sail. They were the sea-castles of the wealthiest maritime empire on earth. Such ships, in the middle of the sixteenth century, were by themselves the emblems and advertisements of national power. They carried sets of gorgeously decorated sails to spread for show, and displayed all manner of heraldic flags and streamers at every possible point. Artists of the time who made official pictures of them usually exaggerated their sheer height above the waterline, with sails and masts such as they could not have carried in reality on such a hull without the ship keeling over in the slightest breeze. But it gave a powerfully fortress-like effect in the pictures, as we may see in a contemporary painting at Hampton Court, showing Henry VIII setting sail with his fleet from Dover in 1520 (see plate 38), to meet the King of France at Calais, at the field of the Cloth of Gold.

Henry VIII was the true founder of the British Navy. Before his time ships in war had been regarded as a sort of floating continuation of the land, where soldiers must somehow contrive to get aboard and fight each other hand to hand; thus they had always been under command of the army. But King Henry now made the navy a separate service, with its own finances, its own repair dockyards, and its own departments for victualling and ordnance, meat, drink, guns, powder and shot. Naval gunnery was a matter in which the English were soon to establish their superiority, and when Philip of Spain's wedding galleons anchored off Southampton the English had no need to be so overawed by them as the Spaniards may have hoped.

38. Ships of Henry VIII's fleet leaving harbour, c. 1520.

Elizabeth continued her father's policies in naval matters as in so many other things, and she had the good fortune to have, in charge of building up her fleet, admirals who could see clearly where the English advantage lay. In the sea-war with Spain which smouldered on, disguised as pirate-raids and privateering, throughout her reign until it burst out in the great final battle of the Armada, the Spaniards were hampered (though they did not know it) by their own long practice of sea warfare. They were a Mediterranean power. They fought their enemies there, in the conditions of that inland sea, with great galleys driven by oars and galley-slaves, crunching in with grappling-irons and military boarding parties. Or else they had high-built ships with fore-and-after-castles from which to overtop and shoot down among the enemy alongside. When they later began to build ships for their Atlantic voyages they still had these old ideas at the back of their minds. But the English had other ideas. Their new ships were generally smaller, lower fore and aft, narrower in the beam, and rather deeper in the water (see plate 39). These features made them quicker and easier to manoeuvre, and being slightly deeper in the water gave them a firmer leverage against the wind, which enabled them to sail more closely into it. It also made a steadier platform for aiming guns.

But of course trade and transportation, not warfare, is the principal business of ships. Most ships of all countries were merchant vessels, and were armed only to defend themselves and their cargoes against pirates. Certainly in the long war which Elizabeth's sailors fought against the Spaniards it was often hard to tell the difference between war and piracy. The Spaniards viewed the English sea-captains as pirates, neither more nor less. The English viewed the Spaniards as an enemy power jealously trying to keep the whole wealth of the still mostly undiscovered New World for themselves. What was at issue was exploration, colonization and overseas trade. The principal objective from beginning to end was the same that had sent Columbus to the New World in the beginning: to find a direct sea-way to the Indies, to the Moluccas, the Spice Islands, for the precious trade in pepper, cloves, nutmeg and cinnamon. So long as

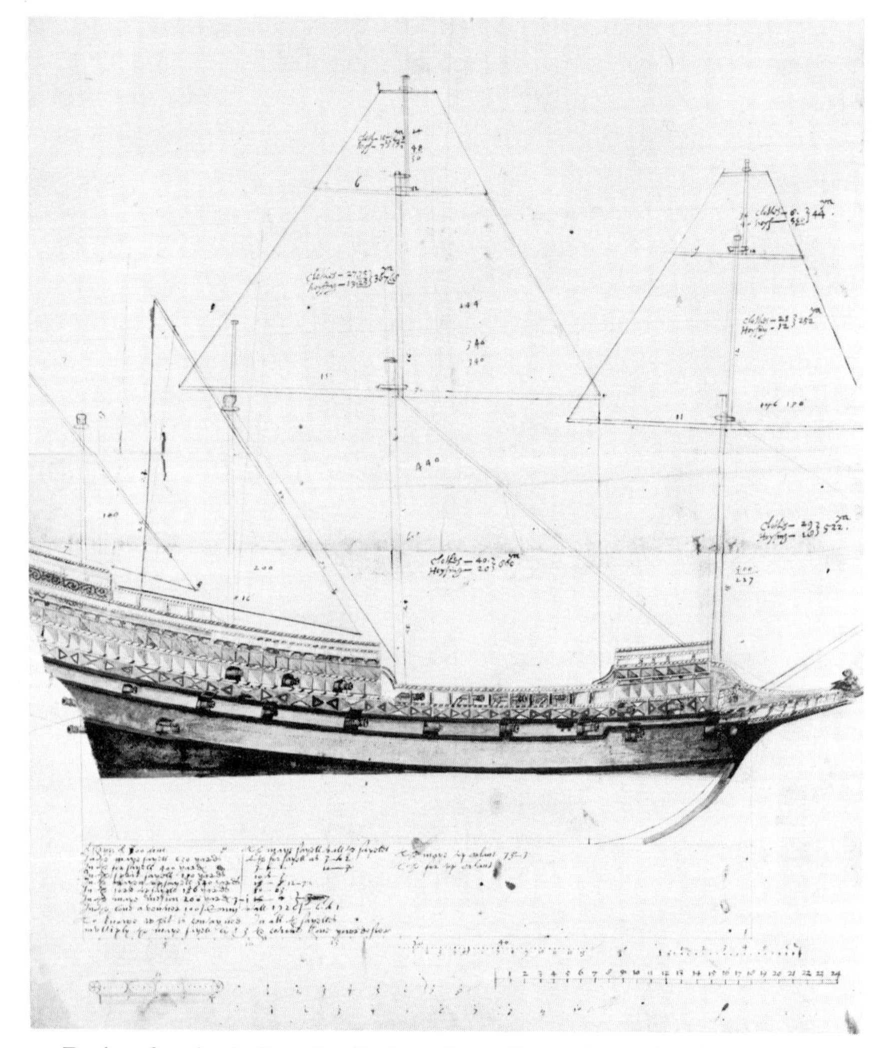

39. Design for the hull and sail-plan of a galleon, drawn by the Elizabethan shipwright Matthew Baker in about 1586. (*See also* plate 41.)

western merchants did not have their own trade-routes, they had to obtain these luxuries at high prices from the Turks of the Eastern Mediterranean, where the Asian caravans came in from across the deserts of Arabia and Turkestan.

To understand why such spices were so much needed, one has to remember how dull, stale and slightly tainted, if not actually bad, was the diet at most people's tables in any great European town such as London during certain parts of the year, especially towards the end of winter. Spices were eagerly sought for, and high prices were paid for small amounts. One ship's cargo could supply a whole town for months, and the shopkeepers could do very well out of it, in a mercantile country such as England was now becoming. The great Spanish treasure convoys, loaded full of gold and silver from America for King Philip's treasury, which the English ships lay in wait to sieze, were in the long run only a spectacular side-issue. In those days, even at a royal table a handful of gold would not do as much as a handful of peppercorns, to make a piece of salt beef, or even venison, palatable at the latter end of February. Trade, not bullion, was the spur.

So during the whole of the sixteenth century rival navigators from the maritime nations of western Europe went probing their way along coastlines hitherto unknown and unimagined, seeking a passage to the East. Five years after Columbus' first voyage to America, John Cabot, a Venetian in the service of Henry VII, sailed out of Bristol for the Indies by way of the North Atlantic. He discovered instead the coasts of Newfoundland and Labrador. Like Columbus before him, he never knew his mistake. Mistakes on such a grand scale are too big to be comprehended all at once. However, before long the navigators Fernan Magellan, for Spain, and Vasco da Gama for Portugal, had opened up the true way to the Indies around the south of Africa and South America; and so for a time Spain and Portugal, could and did claim the great southern oceans for their own. English sailors meanwhile were trying to find a way around in the north, by the supposed North-East and North-West Passages, all without success. With their little wooden ships they ventured in among the icebergs and pack-ice of the Arctic. Some ships were frozen in, some were crushed, none could get through. 'No passage, nor hope of passage' was the concluding verdict of William Baffin on his final return from Baffin Bay. That was in 1616; the dogged search had gone on steadily, even till then. (It continued, on and off, even into the twentieth century.)

The Spanish claim to the southern ocean was not seriously

40. Sir Francis Drake, showing a map of his voyage round the world. Engraving by Crispin van der Passe, 1598.

challenged for nearly sixty years, when Francis Drake (see plate 40) set out from Plymouth in December 1577 to follow Magellan's course into the Pacific. In his ship the *Golden Hinde* (see plate 41), which measured little more than 100 feet long, by 20 feet wide, he made his way through Magellan's Strait during the following autumn. He spent nearly a year raiding Spanish settlements and ships up and down the west coast of South America.

41. The *Golden Hinde*. A modern photograph of a reconstruction of Drake's ship at sea. (*See also* plate 39.)

He landed on the coast of California, which he named Nova Albion, and laid claim to it for England in the queen's name. He seems to have intended to try and find a way home through the North-West Passage from west to east, but failing in this he turned south-west and made for the Moluccas. He stayed there several months trading among the islands, and adding six tons of cloves to the huge cargo of plunder, from no less than forty Spanish ships, which was already stowed, somehow, aboard the *Golden Hinde*. (She ran onto a reef not long after, and some of the cargo had to be thrown overboard to lighten ship and help her off. It was most of the cloves that went.) Then at last he returned to England by way of the Cape of Good Hope and the Atlantic. He arrived home after a voyage of nearly three years. He and his crew were the first Englishmen to sail around the world. By setting up the queen's claim to 'Nova Albion' in California, though in fact he had no hope whatever of establishing it, he was the first Englishman to proclaim an English possession overseas. The cargo he brought back with him was worth (in modern values) some half a million pounds. From his share of it he had made himself a fortune, as well as becoming a national hero. He sailed the *Golden Hinde* up the Thames to Deptford, where Queen Elizabeth came aboard and knighted him there on the deck. A dry dock was built for the *Golden Hinde* at Deptford, where she remained a national monument for a hundred years.

As the century wore on, and as the bewildering disturbances of King Henry VIII's and Queen Mary's time settled down at the fireside with grandfather's memories, English people were able to begin thinking of themselves and their island itself in a quite new, idealized and romantic fashion. They pictured themselves as a heroic people inhabiting a beautiful, peaceful garden, a demi-paradise 'set in the silver sea, which serves it in the office of a wall'. Outside, beyond the wall and the sea, were envious, less happy lands. Chief among these was Spain. The connection with Spain, which had begun happily with the arrival of Catherine of Aragon, had slowly darkened into mutual hostility. Spain now appeared as an open threat to the English nation, the English way of life and the English religion.

To King Philip of Spain the island garden was no paradise, but an embattled fortress of Protestant pirates who plundered his ships and outraged his Catholic faith. In his view (which was shared by Catholics generally) the English queen had not even a legitimate right to the throne. In his view, her father's only lawful wife had been Catherine of Aragon. The daughter of Anne Boleyn could not lawfully be Queen of England. Therefore the rightful queen was Mary Stuart, Queen of Scots (see plate 42), the great niece of Henry VIII and great-granddaughter of Henry VII. Nobody disputed that Mary was in fact the presumptive heir to the English throne, and that if Protestant Elizabeth were to die unmarried and childless, as she was, Catholic Mary would succeed her.

The sad figure of Mary Stuart shadowed the reign of Queen Elizabeth, just as the shadow of Spain hung like a dark cloud over

5. A procession with a dragon (walked along by two men inside). Though this event took place in Brussels it closely resembles what was done in London and other English cities.

6.
The defeat of the Spanish Armada, August 1588. From a contemporary painting.

42. Mary Queen of Scots in 1560.

the English paradise garden. After less than seven years as Queen of Scotland Mary was driven out by insurrection and fled to England. There she was at once put under guard. Without question, her presence in England was a danger to the state. She was a continual focus for conspiracies to kill Elizabeth and put herself on the throne. She certainly knew of these conspiracies and may have been a party to some if not all of them. After the last of these attempts, having been a royal prisoner for nineteen years, she was tried and beheaded. Her death, like a match to a powder train, touched off the great enterprise for the invasion of England which King Philip had for years been considering. Now at last it should be launched.

The story of the Spanish Armada has an epic quality which makes it one of the most remarkable events in the history of warfare. We cannot compress such a quality into a little paragraph, but only make notes. We note the huge fleet of Spanish and Portuguese ships, 130 strong, full of soldiers, setting sail from Lisbon in the early summer of 1588; we note the long watch in England, with the warning beacons ready on the hilltops from one end of the land to the other; the first sighting of the enemy off Cornwall; the English ships working out of Plymouth against the wind to come around behind them; Drake meanwhile finishing his game of bowls on the Hoe; the seven days' fighting up the Channel, towards the Spanish army in the Netherlands waiting for the Armada ships to come and ferry it over the narrow seas to England; the English fire-ships driving in amongst the anchored Spaniards by night; the great sea-battle off the Flemish coast, in a rising gale, the high Spanish fortress-ships trying to grapple the nimble English, who stand off, their guns red hot with continual firing; then the flight of the Spaniards the only way they can go, northward; their stormy voyage home around the north of Scotland, their crippled ships stranding and wrecking one by one along the coasts of the Hebrides and the west of Ireland, having turned southward again; and the return home of hardly more than half their number, during the autumn (see colour plate 6).

The English did not at first realise that their victory was complete. They thought the Armada would return and try again to bring the Spanish army over from Holland. Queen Elizabeth reviewed her army encamped at Tilbury in expectation of an enemy landing, ten days after the Armada had in fact gone forever. But then the clouds lifted and they could see from their battlements the wide empty sea of which they were the masters, and the garden which they could now cultivate in peace.

If ever the Tudor English wished to fancy themselves holding some heroic place alongside the legends of King Arthur's time, here, perhaps, in the epic of the Armada, they might have found it. They were certainly now taking a great pride in the exploits of their seafaring heroes. In the year immediately following the defeat of the Armada, there appeared the first edition of a new book by a certain Richard Hakluyt: *The Principal Navigations, Voyages and Discoveries of the English Nation.* Hakluyt was a geographer, and his purpose was to publicise English exploration and to encourage colonization overseas, especially in North America. He continued working on his book till eventually it filled three volumes. It has the epic scale, and heroes enough to set beside Malory's *Morte d'Arthur*; but Hakluyt's heroes are in the field of history and real life.

IN THE PLEASURE GARDEN

THERE is a miniature painting of an elegant, fashionably dressed young man standing among sprays of roses, leaning as if in poetic thought against a tree, with his hand on his heart (see colour plate 7). It was painted at about the time the Armada was setting sail for England. It beautifully represents the cultivated style which, hand in hand with courage and military adventurousness, were held to be the proper qualities of a noble courtier in the heyday of Queen Elizabeth's reign. The courtier who was the perfect example of these qualities, in the view of all who knew him, was Sir Philip Sidney, the soldier poet whose early death, after a battle against the Spaniards in the Netherlands, was itself renowned for the episode of his sacrificing his last dearly needed drink of water to another wounded soldier whom he considered needed it more than he. Though the young man among the roses is not in fact Sidney, the miniature of another young man, in a rather strange hat, seated near an elaborately laid out garden with a covered walk and a wall around it, and a country house in the background (see plate 43), is sometimes said to be. If it is, it must have been painted a year or two after Sidney's death, when his poems were being printed for the first time. (They had not been written for publication, but as a private gentlemanly exercise, for his pleasure, and to share with his friends.)

The miniature of the young man with the roses is by Nicholas Hilliard. The other is by his follower, Isaac Oliver; and of the two only Hilliard was a native born Englishman. He had based his

43. A young man seated near a formal garden. Miniature by Isaac Oliver, c. 1590.

style upon a study of the work of Hans Holbein. With very few exceptions, all significant pictorial work in England had been, was being, and was yet to be done by artists from abroad, since the days of Holbein until the time of Van Dyck and Rubens in the next century. Against most of the portraits of the great Tudors, and under the illustrations in Tudor books, will be found the names of Dutch painters and engravers (see plate 44). Hilliard was the great exception, great out of all proportion to the miniature size of his works.

Sir Philip Sidney was only twenty-one in the year 1575 when the Earl of Leicester entertained the queen at Kenilworth, and very likely he was present among her courtiers to enjoy the 'Princely Pleasures' there. But in the years that followed his name is most often associated with another great country house, Wilton, near Salisbury, where his sister the Countess of Pembroke lived. Wilton became renowned as a centre for the patronage of music and the arts. Sidney wrote a long pastoral romance there, called *Arcadia*, full of 'meadows enamelled with eye-pleasing flowers', and with the 'shepherd's boy piping, as though he should never be old' (see plate 45). He also wrote a sonnet sequence, *Astrophel and Stella*, following the example of Sir Thomas Wyatt. *Arcadia* he left unfinished, but it was completed by his sister, and published, as were his sonnets, after his death. The seal was set upon the romantic 'arcadian' manner by the poet Edmund Spenser, whose *Shepheardes Calendar* was published in 1579, and dedicated to Sir Philip Sidney.

After Sidney's untimely death his place as a romantic figure among the gallant young men at the queen's court was filled for a time by the young Walter Raleigh. He also, like Sidney, visited Edmund Spenser, and found him at work on his long narrative poem entitled *The Faery Queen*. Raleigh brought Spenser to court, where he read his poem, and heard it proclaimed by one and all the great English epic poem that had been so long awaited. It is an epic patterned like an embroidery with flowers suitable for a battlement garden, and inhabited by heroic figures from the romances of Christian chivalry and classical legend. A sound of music floats in the air of the garden, as if it were a paradise:

44. Title page to *Poly-Olbion* by Michael Drayton, a descriptive poem in praise of the various counties in Britain. This engraving is exceptional, being by an English artist, William Hole; it depicts Great Britain as a goddess of fruit and flowers.

Right hard it was for wight which did it hear
To read what manner music that might be,
For all that pleasing is to living ear
Was there consorted in one harmony,
Birds, voices, instruments, winds, waters all agree.

The joyous birds, shrouded in cheerful shade
Their notes unto the voice attempred sweet;
Th'Angelical soft trembling voices made
To th'instruments divine respondence meet:
The silver sounding instruments did meet
With the base murmur of the water's fall:
The water's fall with difference discreet,
Now soft, now loud unto the wind did call:
The gentle warbling wind low answered to all.

45. An 'arcadian' shepherd and his gear: part of a black-thread embroidery, probably worked by a romantic young lady as a gift for her lover, showing him dressed for the part (late sixteenth century).

Sir Walter Raleigh gathered around him, as Sidney had done, a group of writers and thinkers, of whom one of the foremost was the young playwright, Christopher Marlowe. But whereas Sidney had been chivalrous and, indeed, flattering in what he wrote, Raleigh was, instead, often critical and rash. He and his circle of friends were suspected of atheism, and they were sometimes known as The School of Night. Marlowe was not yet thirty when he was killed in a tavern brawl. People thought that he had lived a raffish and sinister life, and that his fate, like the fate of Dr Faustus in one of his own plays, was something he had brought upon himself. Faustus had sold his soul to the devil in exchange for a few years of worldly power and knowledge. He is seen in the play proudly questioning the devil about the nature and movement of the planets in the heavens:

> Tell me, are there many heavens above the moon?
> Are all celestial bodies but one globe,
> As is the substance of this centric earth?

But at the end of the play, with his time running out, those same heavens roll him on towards his doom. He cries to them for mercy:

> Stand still, you ever-moving spheres of heaven,
> That time may cease, and midnight never come....

But that cannot be. The impious man from the School of Night must stay for his punishment:

> The stars move still, time runs, the clock will strike,
> The devil will come, and Faustus must be damned.

Which is what happened. Faustus and Marlowe and even Sir Walter Raleigh came to unhappy ends, and people sadly shook their heads about them.

The figures of romantic, arcadian poetry, or even the dark criticism of The School of Night, belonged in essence to the life of cultivated people, to the queen and her circle, or to the rash Sir Walter Raleigh and his. But the figures of music, as, for example the musical settings of the services in church, were for

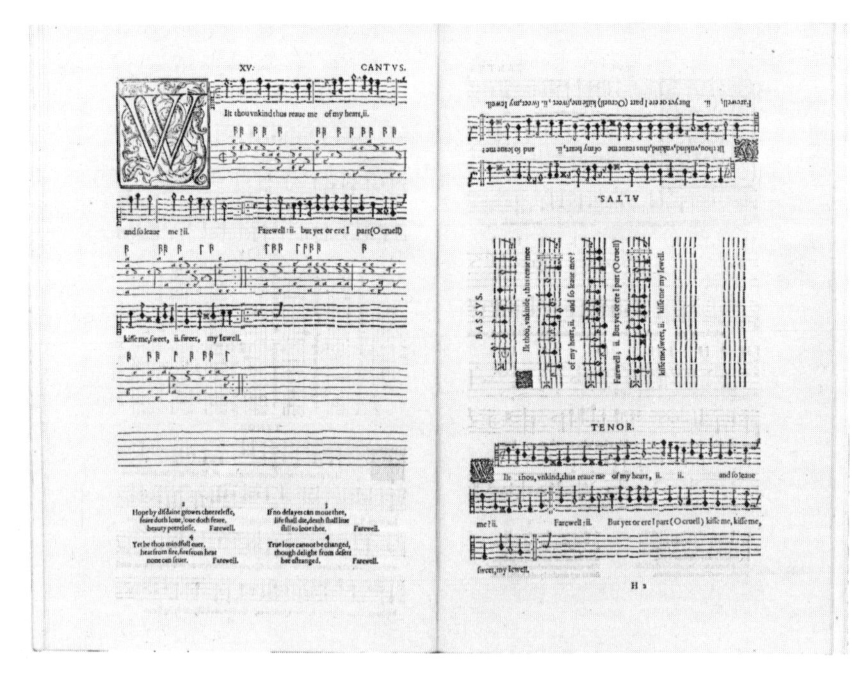

46. A songbook with the different parts laid out for singers sitting round a table. The song is by John Dowland.

everybody. Old Thomas Tallis who as a young man in King Henry's day had helped to establish these settings, had lived to be very old. With his young assistant William Byrd he had published (for now the printers were able to print musical notation) a book of motets in the Kenilworth year of 1575. Since then Byrd and a new generation of young composers had brought English church music to a point of such pre-eminence that it was said that not even the music of the Sistine Chapel in Rome could equal it. And besides this, to read music and to be able to sing it, following one's part in the singing of catches and madrigals, was beginning to be a pleasure in which all members of an ordinary, well-educated family were supposed to be able to join, when the part-books were handed around after supper (see plate 46). The madrigal was originally an Italian musical form, which had been introduced into England by a certain Nicholas Yonge in 1588 (the Armada year, again). The most famous collection of English madrigals, combining as it did the pleasures of English lyric poetry with the equal pleasures of English music by Morley, Gibbons, Weelkes and many others was published with the title *The Triumphs of Oriana*. Oriana was a romantic title for Queen Elizabeth, who herself excelled as a player upon the virginals, the delicate-sounding forerunner of the harpsichord and the piano. The English composers of her time were, among other distinctions, the first founders of the world of keyboard music.

YOUNG MEN IN LONDON

BOYS usually left the grammar school at the age of fifteen or sixteen. Richard Field was eighteen when he was apprenticed to a printer, a certain Thomas Vautrollier, in the Blackfriars neighbourhood in London. In the two years between school and London he may have spent part of the time failing to settle down as cheerfully as his father might have wished in the family tannery business; or he may have begun an apprenticeship with a printer not so far away from his home in Stratford. But at all events, by the year 1579 he was in London.

London at that time was one of the three largest cities in the world (the other two were Naples and Constantinople) and it was still growing rapidly (see plate 47). It had a population of 250,000, more than three times what it was at the beginning of the century when Catherine of Aragon was married there to Prince Arthur; and of course the bigger the city grew, the more attractive it became. London offered an opening to every avenue of opportunity. Ambitious young men flocked into it from every quarter; young lawyers to study at the Inns of Court, young gallants to be in with the fashion, young adventurers to venture themselves and their money in the busiest merchant seaport upon the busiest sea-highway in the world, young scholars from the universities seeking patronage for themselves as writers, to be near the thriving bookshops, where, among other things, they might hope to catch the attention of some rich patron from one of the great houses along the Strand between the City and the

47. An everyday street scene in London. Note the cows, the child with the hoop, the woman selling bread from a basket, the market tables etc. Detail from J. C. Visscher's view of London, 1616.

queen's palace at Whitehall; and now here came young Richard Field, to seek his fortune in the printing trade (see plate 48).

Blackfriars, where Thomas Vautrollier had his printing shop had in the old days been a Dominican monastery. In the great hall there, called the Parliament Chamber, Catherine of Aragon had once stood to answer for herself before King Henry, in her trial for divorce. At the Dissolution the monastery buildings had been divided into different lots and sold off, mostly as private lodgings. In 1576 a whole upper floor was converted into a small theatre by the master of the choirboys of the Chapel Royal. (He put on private performances of plays there, for the gentlemen of the court circle and their friends, during the winter months when the court was in London, using the choirboys for actors.) The out-buildings of the monastery were doubtless sold

48. A printer's trade mark. (*See also* plate 2.)

for storehouses and workshops, and Vautrollier may possibly have had one of them for his printing shop.

The household of a master craftsman was a busy little community, with the master himself and his wife and children, his apprentices and the maids and other servants living all together under one roof; workshop, market-stall, office, training-college and family home, all in one. The master ruled it like a biblical patriarch. Within his house and shop, his word was law; but *he* was ruled by the Master and Court of his trade company or Guild, who laid down the law for the standards and conduct of their trade. He was also governed by an Act of Parliament (The Statute of Artificers, of 1563) which had been brought in to ensure, among other things, that masters would treat their apprentices properly. He was fully responsible for an apprentice's board and lodging, and for giving him a thorough training in every branch of his 'mystery'. He was paid a premium for this by the boy's parents, and the boy was then bound to him in service for a fixed number of years, usually about seven. When he had finished his time the apprentice had to appear before a panel of the Masters of the Company to be examined in the trade and to demonstrate his skill by producing a piece of his work – his 'masterpiece'. If he passed this examination he was then free to set up as a master in his own right, or else to take employment as a journeyman, that is, a 'day-man', working for a master at an agreed daily rate.

A great merchant city such as London naturally contained many thousands of apprentices, and a crowd of them in a festive mood on a public holiday could and often did become boisterous to the point of public disorder. They could all too easily group themselves into street or trade gangs, and were great provokers of brawls and riots. The masters were therefore bound by their Guild laws and by the City Council to keep their apprentices under control, and impose a general code of discipline. Apprentices were not allowed to wear bright or stylish clothes, but must dress in a sober blue colour called watchet, or in russet, or natural wool; and for fabrics only fustian or worsted, canvas or leather. They had to wear plain shirts without ruffs or embroidery, and on their heads the round, flat, woollen cap which was the identifying headgear of the city tradesman.

So Richard Field was housed, fed and lived his life at Vautrollier's; and so he learned the printing trade, and the bookselling trade as well, for the printers naturally worked hand in glove with the booksellers. From Vautrollier's stockroom the bound volumes would be wrapped in cloth and carried up in heavy baskets to the shops in Paul's churchyard. There was the centre of the book market, every shop under its own sign, hanging out like banners over a camp, John Danter at the sign of the Gun, Thomas Heyes at the Green Dragon, Andrew Wise at the Angel, and so on. Field later sold his own books at the sign of the White Greyhound, and so possibly Vautrollier may have done before him.

Paul's Churchyard was (and still is) the name of the street on the south side of the great Cathedral church. In the days before printing there used to be a steady trade outside the church for handwritten prayer sheets – Creeds, Ave Marias and Paternosters — and for rosaries and other such things. The sellers of these pious things each had his own little stall or 'station' in the church precinct, and so they had become known as 'stationers'. With the coming of printing they eagerly turned to selling printed sheets and pamphlets, and then books, and soon they were established in permanent shops around the Churchyard and in nearby Paternoster Row. In 1557 the booksellers, publishers and printers were incorporated as the Stationers Company, with their headquarters at Stationers Hall.

A bookseller could not have had a better centre for his trade than St Paul's and its precinct. The cathedral was the landmark of London, the social meeting place of the city, a public piazza where everybody went to meet their friends for a stroll up and down Paul's Walk at midday, the fashionable hour before dinner. Paul's Walk was the nave of the cathedral. There was no dim religious light or solemn hush under that high vault within the wide open doors, but a constant chatter among groups of people who had their favourite meeting places, beside such or such a pillar, or by some well-known tomb. The best known rendezvous tomb was one generally (but mistakenly, as it happened) thought to be that of Humphrey, Duke of Gloucester, where for some reason needy men used to gather, to beg the price of a meal from acquaintances passing by. 'To dine with Duke Humphrey' was a common expression for being hard up and hungry. At certain pillars men seeking casual employment would wait around to be hired; at others people might paste up trade bills and notices. There were a great many announcing forthcoming plays at the new playhouse recently put up in Shoreditch, a mile outside the city gate on the north. It was called The Theatre. Opinion was divided about it, and some thought it shocking to post playbills in Paul's Walk, which was, after all, a church.

The great steeple of Paul's, the highest in the land, alas, was now no more. It had been struck by lightning in 1561, the year Richard Field was born. The booksellers in Paul's Churchyard had good cause to talk about it still. They had all been afraid their houses would be burned down. The lightning had struck the spire just below the cross. A fire started in the timbers and spread rapidly all the way downwards, the whole structure cracking and twisting and falling apart in blazing fragments which as they dropped set light to the cathedral roofs below. The huge impending pillar of fire blazed for four hours,

7. A young man among roses.
Miniature (here enlarged) by Nicholas Hilliard,
c. 1588.

8. George Clifford, Earl of Cumberland, in his armour as Queen's Champion. Painting by Nicholas Hilliard.

getting itself ready to fall on the houses all around. People could do nothing but fill buckets and barrels with water brought from the public conduits, or carried in relays up the hill from the river, and hope, if the worst came to the worst, their efforts would at least prevent too wide a spread of flame. In all this enormous city of crowded wooden houses there was no trained fire brigade, but only the desperate help of neighbours in time of need. Fortunately this time the houses were all saved. The fire consumed only the cathedral itself, which was gutted to a stone shell. The event was treated as a national calamity. A public subscription for rebuilding the roof was opened at once. The queen contributed a thousand gold marks, and a thousand loads of timber from her own woods. But the great steeple was never rebuilt. John Stow, the historian of London, who saw it all, said that the money for it was collected, 'but little else was done, through whose default God knoweth'.

Along with the ever present danger of fire in the tunnel-streeted, candle-lit, wooden-housed city, went an ever-increasing shortage of fresh water. Fetching it in buckets from the public wells and conduits was a daily chore in most households, and there were water-carriers who went their rounds with it as a trade. There was of course the river Thames, though that was used for so many things it was hardly the cleanest of supplies, and a difficulty was simply how to pump the water up from it into the town. Then in the 1580's an enterprising Dutchman named Peter Morris managed (not without difficulty) to persuade the Lord Mayor and Aldermen of the City to lease him two of the arches of London Bridge, against the north bank. The current of water under the Bridge was very powerful, and Morris used it to drive a series of water-wheels which worked a pump to raise water to a cistern, on a tower high enough to give a head-pressure of water in pipes over a large part of the City. Morris's water-works continued to supply London with piped water for three hundred years.

London Bridge (see plate 49) with its continuous street of shops and houses along the whole length of it (except in one place where an old drawbridge, now no longer capable of being raised, made a short opening in the line) was one of the wonders of Europe. At

49. Old London Bridge. Detail from J. C. Visscher's view of London. 1616.

Alhallowes Berking
Hackney
Billins gate
Bridge Gate

the Southwark end one entered it through a stone gateway, above which on the battlements, was a cluster of poles with the severed heads of executed traitors spiked upon them. They remained till they rotted away, so with time a considerable number were collected there above the gate. This grisly exhibition was a permanent feature which all visitors were taken to gaze at. Londoners only noticed when a new one was added from time to time.

The bridge stood across the tidal stream like nothing so much as a great dam with open sluices. Its nineteen bulky stone piers, standing upon curious rubble-filled platforms called 'starlings', filled up more than half the river. For this reason the current of water forcing its way under the arches was extremely strong, especially when the stream and tide together were flowing out. That was all very fine for Morris's waterworks, but it could be very dangerous for boatmen without experience. The best time to pass under the bridge was at slack water. At the top of the tide one went through like a bullet from a gun.

All along the river on both banks were 'stairs', landing-places where the watermen gathered like taxis at a taxi-rank to pick up passengers, calling 'Eastward ho!' or 'Westward ho!' according to whether they were on their way up or down stream. The river was London's main highway, the chief bringer of all its trade and traffic. It is said that in Queen Mary's time, the Lord Mayor and Aldermen having angered her by a polite but firm refusal over some matter, she had threatened to remove the royal court permanently to some other, more compliant part of her realm. While regretting this the Aldermen were nevertheless overheard to say that so long as she would not take the river Thames away, they might happily survive the loss.

The surface of the river was lively not only with numerous skiffs and wherries, but with flocks of white swans; and beneath the surface was a plenitude of fish, especially eels. They all had plenty to feed on. A flowing river is a great temptation for someone with a bucket of garbage. The butchers' district of Eastcheap had a short way down to the river called (then as now) Pudding Lane. Puddings in those days meant the entrails of slaughtered animals, and the riverside end of Pudding Lane seems to have been where the butchers dumped it all.

It was to be another three hundred years before the skills of science and civil government together could evolve the effective systems of public health upon which the urban civilization of our own time depends. Without it we could not now survive. In Tudor times great cities like London lived perpetually on the edge of risks to life and health which they hardly perceived, except when, occasionally, an outbreak of some epidemic broke through a crack in the thin crust of luck which protected their normal daily lives. The dreaded plague was always, so to speak, just under the floor or around the corner. Some years it came, most years not, or not much of it. They did not know the scuttling rats with their fleas carried it. Doctors could do little or nothing about it. Medicine in those days was in any case, as a profession, mostly a holus-bolus of herbalized witchcraft, astrology, trial and error, blunt surgery, and hopeful quackery sprinkled with Latin. The only real defence against the plague, whenever one heard it had broken out, was, if one could, to get out of town. But most people could not; and in any case more people were always coming into London than ever went out of it.

In the middle of all this Richard Field lived through his apprentice years. Towards the end of his time his master, old Vautrollier, died. A year later Richard married the old man's widow and took over the business. That was in 1588, the year of the Armada, a successful year all round. His was yet one more version of the exemplary citizen's story, the virtuous apprentice, the local boy who made good, in the classic citizen's way. In later life he became Master of the Stationers Company, a very worthy citizen indeed.

But he was by no means the only local boy from Stratford who was making good in those days. Young William Shakespare had recently arrived in London, in pursuit of his own fortune. What had been happening to him while Field was following the path of the industrious apprentice, we do not know. We know that he was married and had three children already, back in Stratford; and that his father after his years of civic eminence, seems to have fallen on harder times. Now in London William was at work in a profession which Richard Field may have had some doubts about: he had become a writer and general factotum for the Theatre in Shoreditch, and sometimes (so Field heard) at that other player-house over on Bankside, the Rose. Field knew a number of these playwriters by sight, and an out-at-elbows, shifty lot he thought them. They came into his shop in Paul's Churchyard, at the sign of the Greyhound, and stood around reading his books for nothing, with their purses in their hands as if they had it in mind to buy something, which they rarely if ever did. Young Shakespeare, though, he had to admit seemed a different case. He simply came in as a friend and an old schoolfellow, to talk about books and writing. He had bought himself a copy of Raphael Holinshed's *Chronicles*, at the publisher's shop not far away. He needed it (and had paid cash for it, he said: where had such money come from?) because he was writing a set of stage plays concerning the history of King Henry VI and the Wars of the Roses, and the defeat of wicked King Richard by good Henry Tudor at the battle of Bosworth, back in grandfather's time. A strange notion, hardly decent, to bring people's own ancestors back to life, so to speak, upon the public stage. He invited Shakespeare upstairs into the house, to talk about these things out of hearing of the apprentices. He did not want those lads sneaking off again, as two of them had recently done, all one afternoon over the river to see the play about Doctor Faustus and the Devil, by Christopher Marlowe, a reputed atheist and therefore undoubtedly a bad example for young men. As a master craftsman, though still not very old himself, he had his apprentices' morals, to say nothing of his own business, to look after.

Here now in London of a sudden, like the rising of a new sun, a new profession was emerging, that of the *professional* theatre with its own purpose-built playhouses – the first commercial playhouses ever built by actors for their own uses – filled every day with new audiences eager for new plays. Combined with this was the spread of leisure-reading by a new class of readers – for, with the increase of printing and cheaper books, reading was no longer a luxury for noble, learned or privileged people. All this offered plentiful opportunities for a new class of young men from the grammar schools and universities seeking to make their way in the world by yet another new profession, the *profession* of literature. The host of writers whose names suddenly appeared in the theatres and bookshops of London, in the years after the Armada, were the sons not of landowners and noble families, but of clergymen, lawyers, shoemakers, bricklayers, linendrapers, leather-sellers, scriveners and clerks. From these tradesmen's shops came William Shakespeare, Christopher Marlowe, Ben Jonson and all the other writers who made the Elizabethan age one of the most remarkable episodes in the history of western culture. The battlement garden was green and coming into flower. It was the modern world beginning.

THE WORLD A STAGE

WHENEVER, during its summer visitations, the plague in London caused more deaths than usual (variously estimated at between thirty and fifty a week) the City Corporation at once ordered all the playhouses to be closed. The Corporation was always ready to seize a convenient excuse for closing playhouses, which they regarded as centres of general idleness and disorder; but whether or not they had justification at other times, in plague time the precaution was certainly wise. To have so many people crowded together in one place for two or three hours at a stretch was certain to spread the contagion. The closures, however, only lasted so long as the infection was at its height, and the playhouses were usually back in business again after a week or two. Moreover there were four pleasant years from the Armada year of '88 until the end of 1591 when there was hardly any infection at all, and in that freedom the playhouses thrived.

But then in 1592 the plague returned with a quite unusual virulence, which continued unabated for three years. The noblemen in their great houses along the river closed them up and went off to the safety of their country estates. The queen and her court stayed away from Whitehall. The playhouses, of course, were shut up fast, and remained so for the whole three years. It looked for a time as if the acting profession in London was at an end. The player companies were obliged to pack up and tour the country towns again, as they had used to do in the old days. There still exists a homesick letter written by a famous actor, Edward

Alleyn, while he was away on tour in Bristol, to his wife, who had had to remain with the family in London. He calls her his 'good sweet Mouse', and says he hopes in God 'though the sickness be round about you yet, by His Mercy, it may escape your house'. He advises her as a precaution to keep the house 'fair and clean', to wash down the forecourt and back yard with water every evening, and to keep sweet herbs at all the windows. He then goes on to ask about 'domestical matters, such things as happen at home, as how your distilled water proves, or this, or that, or any other thing what you will'. He asks after his garden, and gives her instructions for sowing the spinach. 'I would do it myself, but we shall not come home till Allholland* tide. And so, sweet mouse, farewell, and brook our long journey with patience.'

William Shakespeare (see plate 50) had begun to make his name as a dramatist in the three lucky years between the plagues. His four plays about the Wars of the Roses (the three parts of *Henry VI*, and *Richard III*) had proved very popular. Their purpose was to demonstrate on the public stage all the cruelties and confusions of those dreadful times, and how the country had at last been saved from them by Henry VII, Queen Elizabeth's grandfather. In the confident years following the defeat of the Armada, that was just what the great playgoing public was eager to see and hear. But it seems also that, besides the theatre audiences, quite early in his career Shakespeare had made friends in high places. One of these was the young Earl of Southampton, who at that time was in great favour at Court. The Earl had made a reputation for himself as a patron of literature and the arts. So when in 1592 the theatres were closed by the plague, Shakespeare had another string to his bow. He laid aside playwriting for a while, and set himself to composing two long, elegant narrative poems on classical themes, *Venus and Adonis* and *The Rape of Lucrece*, which he dedicated to the earl (' . . . if your Honour seems but pleased, I account my selfe highly praised . . .'). It is thought Shakespeare may have spent some part of the plague years staying at the earl's country estate in Hampshire, and

* All Hallows. (November 1st.)

MR. WILLIAM
SHAKESPEARES
COMEDIES,
HISTORIES, &
TRAGEDIES.

Publiſhed according to the True Originall Copies.

LONDON

Printed by Iſaac Iaggard, and Ed. Blount. 1623.

50. William Shakespeare. A likeness agreed by friends who knew him, and who used it for the title page of his collected works.

indeed the poems may have been written there. What is certain is that both of them were printed by Shakespeare's friend Richard Field, and were 'to be sold at the sign of the White Greyhound in Paules Church-yard.' In fact they sold very well and were reprinted many times. Strangely enough, they are believed to be the only ones of all Shakespeare's works of which the printer's proofs may have been seen and corrected by the poet himself.

It was around this time that Shakespeare wrote *A Midsummer Night's Dream.* It is a play that has all the indications of having been written to celebrate an important wedding at a nobleman's house, where it would have been acted in the great hall. It happens that just such a wedding took place in January 1595, when the young Earl of Derby married the daughter of the Earl of Oxford. Both these noblemen were patrons of player companies. The bridegroom's family, in particular, had for many years been patrons of the company to which Shakespeare himself belonged; so it is possible that Bottom with his asses head, and Puck and Oberon and Titania made their first appearance before him and his bride at the family home of the Earl of Oxford. We may imagine a very noble gathering of wedding guests, for the bride was the granddaughter of no less a person than old William Cecil, Lord Burghley himself, the queen's lifelong and most trusted counsellor.

By the spring of 1595 the plague had burnt itself out. London was free of it once more. The playhouses re-opened their doors, the actors returned, and the audiences flocked in to see them as never before. Foreign visitors were always curious to see these strange theatres, for no other city in the world had anything like them. A new one called the Swan had recently been built on Bankside, and a Dutch visitor wrote home to a friend that it was big enough to hold 3000 people. Even if he was exaggerating it is still certain that audiences at the theatres could be very large, especially as a large proportion of them were standing, and at a popular play they could be packed in very tightly together. Such crowds offered golden opportunities for pickpockets, though if one was caught at it the custom was to tie him up to a post on the stage, where apple cores and rubbish could be thrown at him all the afternoon. Plays might be popular, but they were not always listened to with noiseless attention. The crowds on Bankside were a strange mixture of brutishness and refinement. Next door to the playhouse was the animal-baiting ring, where you might see a poor bear, chained to a stake, being torn about by savage dogs. The 'sport' was to see how long the maddened bear could last it out, or how many dogs he could kill, and to lay wagers on it all. It seems that the puritans, but only they, were disgusted by such entertainments (as they were also by play-acting), and when on one occasion an over-crowded gallery at a bear-baiting collapsed onto the people below, killing many of them, the preachers made much of it from their pulpits, pointing out that it was a punishment for sin; for it had happened on a Sunday when the people should have been at church.

The big public playhouses were built in a very similar way to the bear-baiting rings (see plate 51). They were open arenas, usually circular, surrounded by wooden galleries three stories high. The gallery part was roofed with thatch, but the arena, or yard, was open to the sky. Into the middle of this yard, thrust out from one side, was a big rectangular stage, somewhat like a very high table. At the back of this, over against the galleries, was a screen wall with two or three openings in it, fitted with doors and curtains, through which the actors came out onto the stage. Their 'backstage' area, behind the screen wall, they called the 'tiring-house' (that is the place where they attired themselves in their costumes). Over the stage itself there was a sort of roof, to keep the showers off the actors and their stage properties in unsettled weather: the audience standing around them in the yard would put up with a shower or two, to save expense, for it cost more to go into the galleries (where one might also have a seat). It was a simple arrangement, not unlike the inn-yards where the players in the country towns still used to perform; and at least one theatre manager 'doubled-up' his playhouse by having a portable stage which could be taken away so that the arena space could also be used for bear-baiting.

A simple arrangement, but not bare, meagre or unattractive. As soon as the actors were able to settle down in their own play-

51. A public playhouse: the audience assembling and the play about to begin. Note some of the audience seated on the stage, others standing in the yard. (A modern reconstruction drawing.)

houses they were able to collect a handsome store of costumes, curtainings, thrones and chariots and other stage furniture. The playhouses, inside, were painted and decorated in such a way that their puritan critics, shocked as usual, complained about the gorgeous extravagance of them, and called them 'Venus palaces'.

Be that as it may, a reading of any of Shakespeare's plays will show what a deal of elegant and sometimes complicated furnishing is required in order to put it on the stage at all. Though he neither had nor needed the scenic apparatus customary in most modern theatres, his stage was by no means bare.

In spite of every sort of disapproval and restraint by preachers, puritanical persons and city authorities, the theatre as an institution was continually increasing in popularity among all classes of people. By the end of the century London had no less than seven permanent playhouses in operation, not counting inn-yards still occasionally used by visiting companies. In the year 1599 the Company led by the famous actor Richard Burbage, in which Shakespeare worked and was a principal shareholder, built their own new playhouse on Bankside, giving it what is certainly one of the most famous names in theatre history: The Globe. Its picture appears in the foreground of a panoramic view of London published a few years later, labelled in its own right as an important feature of the city, like the Guildhall or St Paul's (see plate 52). (The artist did not get it quite right however. His picture makes it too tall and narrow. Probably he was working from somebody else's sketches.)

Shakespeare in a well-known speech, said that the world is a stage, upon which men and women come and go like actors, playing their different parts and changing their costumes as they grow older and seem to become different people. That speech has always been popular in all languages, because people recognise it as true of themselves. Men and women in their lives are all possessed by imaginative ideas about their own natures, about what becomes them, what is due to them, what they are to each other, and how they ought to behave. The theatre shows us models of the world in action, which people copy as models for themselves. Shakespeare also said that actors even at their best are only the 'shadows' of what they present; but people of our time, watching the shadows on cinema or television screens, should know what a powerful influence upon real life such shadows can have. In Tudor times the sudden expansion of this imaginative power of self-knowledge, of seeing life modelled and

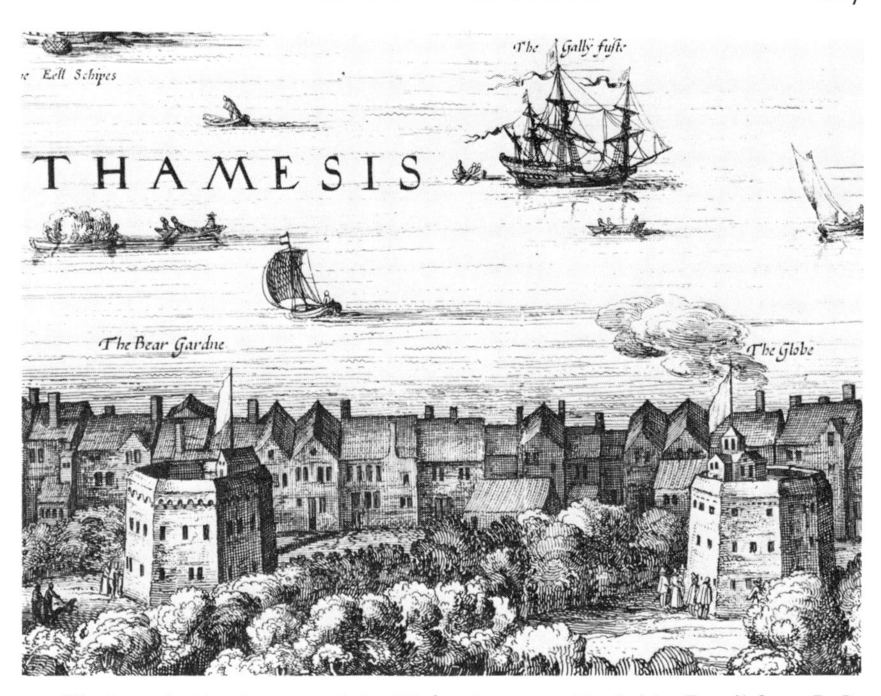

52. The bear-baiting house and the Globe theatre on Bankside. Detail from J. C. Visscher's view of London, 1616.

acted out by skilled professions upon the stage, must have come as a revelation. Moreover, where in former times the cultivated arts had been available only to a few very rich people, now they were served up piping hot for everybody; last night for the queen and her courtiers at Whitehall palace; this afternoon for Jack and and his master at the Globe on Bankside. No wonder the theatre was popular. No wonder religious preachers and civic officials alike suspected it could be an unpredictable and therefore dangerous influence in society, and ought to be suppressed. But it could not be suppressed. The effect had already spread too far. For instance, the player company at the Globe was no longer under the patronage of a private nobleman, but of the queen's Lord Chamberlain himself. (And in the next reign they were patronized directly by the king). They were needed for the festival entertainments of the Court, and were held at the command of the Master of the Revels (see plate 53).

53. The Queen's favourite clown, Richard Tarlton, is drawn here inside an elaborate letter 'T', dancing a jig with his pipe and tabor. Tarlton was the most famous comedian of his generation.

Meanwhile, in addition to their successful new Globe, they had taken over the lease of the old great hall at Blackfriars, the place where Catherine of Aragon had stood her trial, which had been fitted up as an indoor theatre. Thus offering greater comfort, they could attract the patronage of well-to-do gentlemen and their ladies in the evening – the 'carriage trade' in almost literal fact, for people in the neighbouring streets complained a great deal about the noise of all the coaches cluttering up the roads and clattering on the cobbles, bringing in the high-class patrons from the suburbs to Blackfriars.

Young lawyers from the Inns of Court were enthusiastic patrons of the theatre, and, quick to follow the fashion, amused themselves with writing and acting their own plays. The choirmasters of St Paul's and the queen's Chapel Royal had for many years trained their boys in acting as well as singing. Now they set the boys up in direct competition with the famous adult companies. Some of these boys went on to become professional actors, after their voices had broken, as also did many of the boys in the professional companies, who so successfully played all the women's parts. (It would probably have been even more offensive to the actors than to their audiences to have had women taking parts with them upon the stage. Their professional traditions were all against it).

The general enthusiasm for plays was quickly seen in the bookshops. There was a ready demand for copies of the latest works by popular dramatists. However, it was often difficult for printers to get hold of their scripts. These did not belong to the authors, but to the playhouse managers who had bought them outright, and kept them safely locked away in the playhouse strong-box, for fear of pirating by rival managements. There was no law of copyright. Printers therefore would sometimes resort to having new plays taken down in shorthand for them during performances, or they would buy versions repeated from memory by sneaky actors (who, of course, were usually only word-perfect in their own parts). The results of such ploys were at best very uneven, but the need for them shows what opportunities there were in the theatre for new writers to make their livings. Shakespeare, indeed, made more than a living: he made himself a small fortune.

He was among the foremost writers from the moment he first appeared, and was soon ahead of all the others. The young poet who might have rivalled him, Christopher Marlowe, had been killed in a tavern brawl in 1593. The other, Ben Jonson, who certainly wished to rival him and had all the skill to do so, had only the skill, but without Shakespeare's sympathetic warmth of nature. Shakespeare was thrice-gifted: he was a poet of genius who was also a shrewd business man; and into the bargain it seems he had an engaging personality. Everybody liked him.

Going home to Stratford to visit his family, at the turn of the century, still with many of his greatest works ahead of him, he could already be counted a truly successful man. At the age of thirty-five he was the author of some nineteen or twenty famous plays. He was a leading partner in a most profitable enterprise at the Globe playhouse. He had just bought himself a new house in Stratford, one of the finest in the town; and he had obtained for his old father a grant of arms from the College of Heralds, thus conferring upon the retired leather-merchant, in spite of a certain decline of his fortunes in recent years, the right to call himself a Gentleman. His mother, Mary Shakespeare, once Arden, on behalf of all the Ardens of Warwickshire, must have been more than satisfied.

Epilogue: THE NEW CENTURY

A FOREIGN visitor to London in 1598 wrote of the English that they were 'vastly fond of great noises that fill the ear, . . . so that in London it is common for a number of them, that have got a glass in their heads, to go up into some belfry, and ring the bells for hours together, for the sake of exercise'. One suspects that the good foreigner was having his leg pulled by the natives. What he had heard was not a drunken frolic (as he was told)but the local bell-ringers practising their changes. The art of pealing the bells in changes was (and still is) exclusively English, and he would have heard nothing like it at home, or anywhere else. But be that as it may, when one counts the cluster of church towers standing up on the old views of Elizabethan London, one may guess that the bells at midnight, ringing in the new century as the last hour of December of 1599 went out, would indeed have been a great noise that filled the ear.

By then, the lady of the battlement garden had grown old (see plates 54 and 57). Nevertheless she continued vigorously to play her part within the walls that had withstood the mighty Armada, the greatest assault ever made upon her country since the Norman Conquest. The same visitor who had heard the bells in London had a view of her at Greenwich palace, in her old age. He described her as being 'fair but wrinkled', and with black teeth, 'a defect the English seem subject to, from their too great use of sugar'. She was dressed in white silk, 'bordered with pearls of the size of beans'. The occasion was an official reception for foreign

54. Queen Elizabeth: a portrait painted in 1592 to commemorate her visit to Sir Henry Lee at Ditchley in Oxfordshire, where, on the map at her feet, she is standing.

ambassadors, and 'as she went a long in all this state and magnificence, she spoke very graciously, first to one then to another . . . in English, French and Italian; for besides being well skilled in Greek, Latin and the languages I have mentioned, she is mistress of Spanish, Scotch and Dutch. Whoever speaks to her, it is kneeling; now and then she raises some with her hand.'

Her grandfather, Henry VII, had successfully healed and restored a country whose whole political system had been wrecked by thirty years of civil war. He had dressed up his task with a certain quality of poetic imagination: the cultivation of the Tudor rose of red and white, and the idea of a new King Arthur. But behind the dressing he had been shrewd, steady-handed and managerial. It may be said of him that he was the first English monarch to conduct his task in a truly *professional* manner, as if it were itself a skilled job. The same was true of his granddaughter. Thus the Tudor dynasty ended as it began, in the hands of a professional. Queen Elizabeth managed her ministers in a way which often infuriated them, when she seemed to them irrational and quirky. But it is noticeable how loyally they all worked with her, and how rarely she changed them. Like a good director, she knew how to choose the right man for a post, and having done so she would support him to the utmost. It is likely that at least one of the reasons why she remained unmarried was her unwillingness to have a partner in her management. It was not so much her throne she cared about: it was her job.

Looking back on the Tudor age we remember that one of its most striking features is the emergence, as if suddenly entering in their parts upon a stage, of so many women. It is unfortunate that many of their parts (though not all) were tragic ones. But they all appear different, personal, and strongly characterized in their own right. The six wives of Henry VIII do, of course, set the idea off to a notable start. One remembers especially the patient dignity of Catherine of Aragon, followed by the pathetic little tragedy of Anne Boleyn. A tragedy in more sombre colours accompanies the figure of Mary Tudor trying and failing, with her own bitter morality, to right her mother's wrongs. Less tragic, but truly pathetic, is that other Mary, the Queen of Scots. She figures often in historical writing as a beautiful princess, ill-treated and finally slain in a hard, unloving world. That is only partly true. Her trouble was that she was the very opposite of Queen Elizabeth, whose own world, at her beginning, was quite as hard as Mary's became; but Elizabeth could manage her world, where Mary could not. Mary was always seeking to do what Elizabeth refused to do, to put herself and her job into the hands of some capable, managing man; and then she proved very bad at choosing one, which in the end led to her downfall. But it is not only women of royalty who appear so outstandingly upon the scene of Tudor England. Mary Stuart's keeper during most of her captivity in England was the Earl of Shrewsbury, whose wife Elizabeth, familiarly known to history as 'Bess of Hardwick', was a person of a character almost as strong as that of the Queen her namesake. She married and buried four husbands, and amassed a great fortune, much of which she spent building palatial houses in the north of England. It is said she believed she would not die so long as she was building; and she lived firmly into her eighty-seventh year. A portrait gallery of the notable women of that great century could be extended a long way; but in the end all their images are pale beside that of the lady of the battlement garden who now, in the new century, was old.

King Arthur also had grown old. It was a hundred and fifteen years since William Caxton had printed Sir Thomas Malory's book. But the notion of an ideal chivalry and its romances had survived, had even increased in glamour, and was concentrated now around the person of the old queen. In her young days, when she first came to the throne, her subjects had greeted her reign with heartfelt rejoicing and thankfulness. After the unsettled times that had followed old King Henry's death she brought a much needed peace and stability to the kingdom. Then as she aged in the years after the Armada, the people's admiration for her turned into adoration. At court she became the centre of a cult of poetic chivalry. Gallant young men flattered her with romantic names: Cynthia, Astraea, Gloriana. Edmund Spenser's epic poem 'The Faery Queen' was written entirely in this mood of idealized knighthood, in honour of the glory of her reign. Her

55. Tilting at barriers. This form of martial sport, a ceremonial combat on foot, was introduced during the sixteenth century. Note the ornamental armour and pageantry on the arena. (French tapestry, c. 1573.)

courtiers had their tournament armour fashioned and gilded as if to suit a new order of chivalry in a new Camelot. Their shields were painted with allegorical devices, mottoes and emblems whose

56. Original drawings for a suit of armour, with its additional pieces, c. 1565.

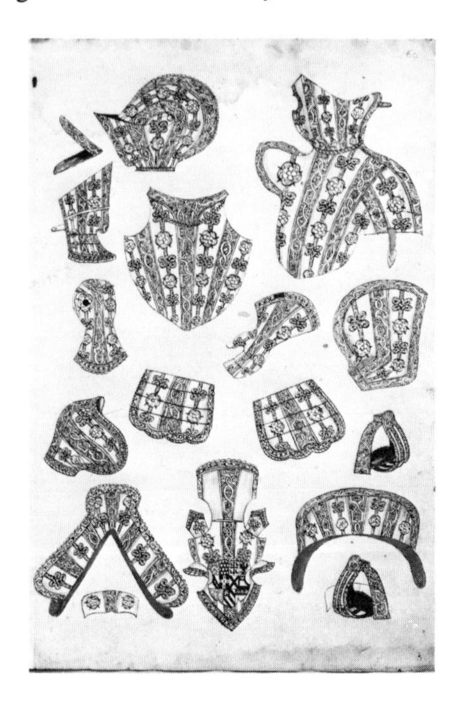

meanings the spectators were supposed to interpret as the knights entered the lists.

Tournaments in the royal tiltyard were highly ornamental occasions (see plate 55). The queen's royal gallery would be dressed to represent the Fortress of Perfect Beauty, or some such noble place, which would have to be defended by the queen's knights against the assaults of a fairy-tale enemy. The armour of the combatants was often surprisingly fanciful. On one occasion two knights appeared 'both in like armour, beset with apples and fruit, the one signifying Adam, the other Eve, who had hair hung all down her helmet'. The Queen's Champion in these tiltyard entertainments for many years was one of her favourite courtiers, Sir Henry Lee, and the pattern drawings for one of his suits of tilting armour still exist (see plate 56). When he grew old there was a touching ceremony in the tiltyard, when he handed over his duties as Queen's Champion to the Earl of Cumberland. Of Cumberland, too, we have a picture, in his pageant armour painted all over with golden stars, and with Queen Elizabeth's glove, her royal favour, pinned to his hat (see colour plate 8). Even in the last year of her reign she did not fail to appear, seated in her royal state, to witness her chivalric 'triumphs' in the tiltyard. Old Gloriana never ceased to take pleasure in these occasions.

We may imagine her, then, in the last year of her life, setting out on a summer's day upon the Thames in her royal barge, leaving the palace at Greenwich and being rowed upstream towards London. They row her past Drake's old ship, the *Golden Hinde,* mouldering in its dry dock at Deptford; past all the merchant ships anchored at the approaches to the greatest merchant city of western Europe; and past the Tower where she had once been held prisoner. (The space on the battlements where she used to take her exercise is to this day called Elizabeth's Walk). At slack water they row her under London Bridge – they had timed her journey carefully with the tide – and beyond it she passes among all the watermen ferrying the playgoers over the river to Bankside. Shakespeare himself perhaps, at the landing place, watches her pass by. At Whitehall Stairs she disembarks, to stay at the Palace there for a night or two. A few days later she will be rowed up-stream again, towards her favourite palace at Richmond.

At Richmond on a dark night in March, 1603, she died, and the dynasty of the Tudors was folded away. All next day the bells in all the church towers of London tolled, and throughout all the land, into Warwickshire, over Arden and beyond to Ludlow Castle, where young Prince Arthur died, the bells tolled and tolled all day long.

57. Queen Elizabeth carried in a litter by the Knights of the Garter, c. 1600.

BIBLIOGRAPHY

1. SOURCE MATERIAL

Burton, Elizabeth. *The Elizabethans at Home.* Longman, Harlow

Byrne, Muriel St Clare. *Elizabethan Life in Town and Country.* Methuen, London, 1925

Gasquet, F. A. *Henry VIII and the English Monasteries.* John Hodges, 1889

Hodges, C. Walter. *Shakespeare and the Players.* G. Bell, London, 1970

—— *Shakespeare's Theatre.* Oxford University Press, London, 1964

Mattingly, Garrett. *Catherine of Aragon.* Jonathan Cape (Bedford History Series), London

—— *The Defeat of the Spanish Armada.* Jonathan Cape, London, 1959 and 1970 (paperback)

Morris, Christopher. *The Tudors.* Batsford, London, 1955 and Collins (Fontana), London, 1966

Neale, J. E. *Queen Elizabeth I.* Jonathan Cape, London, 1934 (Bedford History Series) and 1967 (paperback)

Nichols, John. *The Progresses and Public Processions of Queen Elizabeth* (3 vols). London, 1823

Quennel, Marjorie and C. H. B. *History of Everyday Things in England* (vol. 2). Batsford, London, 1960

Rowse, A. L. *England of Elizabeth.* Sphere (Cardinal), London, 1973

Salzman, L. F. *England in Tudor Times.* Batsford, London, 1926

Trevelyan, G. M. *English Social History.* Longman, Harlow and Penguin, Harmondsworth, 1970

Wilson, John Dover. *Life in Shakespeare's England.* Cambridge University Press, Cambridge, 1920

2. LITERATURE OF THE TIME

Byrne, Muriel St Clare (Ed.). *The Elizabethan Home: Discovered in Two Dialogues by Claudius Hollyband and Peter Erondell.* Methuen, London, 1949

Foxe, John. *Book of Martyrs*. Edited by G. A. Williamson. Secker and Warburg, London, 1965
Hakluyt, Richard. *Selections*. Edited by A. E. Hall. G. Bell, London
Henderson, P. (Ed.). *Shorter Novels* (vol. 1 Elizabethan). Dent, (Everyman Paperbacks), London
Holinshed, Raphael. *Chronicle as Used in Shakespeare's Plays*. Edited by Allardyce and J. Nicoll. Dent (Everyman Library), London
Lucie-Smith, Edward. *The Penguin Book of Elizabethan Verse*. Penguin, Harmonsworth, 1968
McIlwraith, A. K. (Ed.). *Five Elizabethan Comedies*. Oxford University Press, Oxford, 1934
—— *Five Elizabethan Tragedies*. Oxford University Press (Oxford Paperbacks), London, 1971
Malory, Sir Thomas. *Morte d'Arthur* (2 vols). Edited by J. Cowan. Penguin, Harmondsworth, 1969
Marlowe, Christopher. *Complete Plays*. Edited by J. B. Steane. Penguin, Harmondsworth, 1969
Shakespeare, William. *Complete Works*. Edited by Peter Alexander. Collins, London, 1951
Spenser, Edmund. *Poetical Works*. Edited by James Cruickshank Smith and Ernest de Selincourt. Oxford University Press (Oxford Paperbacks), London, 1970
Stow, John. *Survey of London*. Edited by Charles Lethbridge Kingsford. Oxford University Press, London, 1971 and Dent (Everyman Paperbacks), London
Webster, John. *Three Plays*. Edited by David C. Ganby. Penguin, Harmondsworth, 1972

3. FICTION FOR THE SAME AGE GROUP

Bohan, Edmund. *The Buckler*. Hutchinson, London, 1972
Bolt, Robert. *A Man For All Seasons*. Samuel French, London and Heinemann Education, London, 1967
Eldridge, Denise. *The Queen's Choyce*. Macmillan, London, 1974
Harnett, Cynthia. *Load of Unicorn*. Methuen, London, 1959
Hodges, C. Walter. *Playhouse Tales*. G. Bell, London, 1974
Mason, A. E. W. *Fire Over England*. Hodder and Stoughton, London, 1936
Prescott, H. F. M. *Man On a Donkey*. Eyre and Spottiswoode, London, 1953
Sitwell, Edith. *Fanfare for Elizabeth*. Macmillan (paperback), London, 1966
Sutcliffe, Rosemary. *Brother Dusty-Feet*. Oxford University Press, London, 1965
Trease, Geoffrey. *Cue for Treason*. Puffin, Harmondsworth, 1970
Willard, Barbara. *A Cold Wind Blowing*. Puffin, Harmondsworth, 1975
—— *The Iron Lilly*. Puffin, Harmondsworth, 1970

INDEX